10 PEOPLE
Every Christian
Should Know

10 PEOPLE Every Christian Should Know

LEARNING FROM SPIRITUAL GIANTS OF THE FAITH

Warren W. Wiersbe

BakerBooks

a division of Baker Publishing Group
Grand Rapids, Michigan

© 2011 by Warren W. Wiersbe

Published by Baker Books
a division of Baker Publishing Group
P.O. Box 6287, Grand Rapids, MI 49516-6287
www.bakerbooks.com

ISBN 978-0-8010-1542-7

This book is comprised of excerpts from Warren Wiersbe, *50 People Every Christian Should Know* (Grand Rapids: Baker Books, 2009).

Chapters 4, 5, 6, and 10 originally © 1971–1977 by the Moody Bible Institute, reprinted by permission of *Moody Monthly;* chapter 7 originally © 1984, 1985 by Back to the Bible; chapters 1, 2, 3, 8, and 9 originally appeared as articles in *Good News Broadcaster*, copyright by The Good News Broadcasting Association, Inc., Lincoln, NE 68501.

12   13   14   15   16   17   18   7   6   5   4   3   2   1

Contents

1

Matthew Henry
1662–1712

"Suitable to everybody, instructive to all" is the way Charles Spurgeon described what is probably the best-known commentary on the Bible written in the English language, *Matthew Henry's Commentary*.[1] Since it was first published more than two hundred and fifty years ago, this commentary has appeared in many different editions, including a condensation in one volume.

Spurgeon recommended that every minister of the gospel read straight through *Matthew Henry's Commentary* at least once during his lifetime. Perhaps he got this idea from his model, George Whitefield, who carried his set of Matthew Henry on all of his travels and read it daily on his knees.

Matthew Henry was born at Broad Oaks, Shropshire, England, on October 18, 1662. His father, Philip Henry, was a Nonconformist minister who, along with two thousand other clergymen, had been ejected from his church by the Act of Uniformity issued that year by Charles II. These courageous men had refused to compromise their convictions and give "unfeigned consent and assent" to the Prayer Book. They also refused to submit to Episcopal ordination.

Philip Henry had married an heiress of a large estate in Broad Oaks named Catherine Matthews. Her father was not in favor of the match and told his daughter, "Nobody knows where he came from." But Catherine wisely replied, "True, but I know where he is going, and I should like to go with him!"

Matthew was physically weak, but it was not long before his strength of intellect and character made themselves known. At the age of three, he was reading the Bible; by the time he was nine, he was competent in Latin and Greek. He spent his first eighteen years being tutored at home, in an atmosphere that was joyfully and lovingly Christian.

He loved to hear his father preach. A sermon on Psalm 51:17 first awakened in young Matthew a desire to know the Lord personally. He was only ten years old at the time, but the impression was lasting. When he was thirteen, Matthew wrote an amazingly mature analysis of his own spiritual condition, a document that reads like an ordinary paper. Often, after hearing his father preach, Matthew would hurry to his room and pray that God would seal the Word and the spiritual impressions made to his heart so that he might not lose them. God answered those youthful prayers.

In July 1680, Matthew was sent to London to study with "that holy, faithful minister," Thomas Doolittle, who had an academy in his home. Unfortunately, the religious persecutions of the day forced Doolittle to close his academy; Matthew returned to Broad Oaks. In April 1685, he returned to London to study law at Gray's Inn. He was a good student, but he never lost the burning desire to be a minister of the gospel.

A year later he returned to Broad Oaks and began to preach whenever opportunity presented itself, and on May 9, 1687, he was ordained. Before his ordination, he put himself through a heart-searching self-examination in which he seriously studied his own Christian experience, motives for ministry, and fitness for service. The paper contains both confession of faith and confession of sin. He concluded that he was not entering the ministry "as a trade to live by" or to make a name for himself. He also concluded, "I have no design in the least to maintain a party, or to keep up any schismatical faction."

Throughout his ministry, Matthew Henry loved and cooperated with all who trusted Christ and wanted to serve him, no matter what their denominational connections. Even the leaders of the Episcopal Church admitted that Matthew Henry was a good and godly man. This document ought to be read by every prospective minister before he comes to ordination, and it would not hurt those of us who are already ordained to review it on occasion.

A group of believers in Chester invited Matthew Henry to become their pastor, and on June 2, 1687, he began twenty-five happy years of ministry among them. Though he was in demand to preach in other churches in the area, he was rarely absent from his own pulpit on the Lord's Day.

He was married in August of the same year. On February 14, 1689, his wife died in childbirth, although, by the mercy of God, their daughter lived. Matthew married again on July 8, 1690, and God gave him and his wife nine children, eight of them girls, three of whom died during their first year. His only son, Philip, was born May 3, 1700, but he did not follow his father's faith, or his grandfather's. His interests lay in this world and not in the world to come.

God blessed the ministry in Chester so that a new sanctuary was erected and was dedicated on August 8, 1700. The effectiveness of Matthew Henry's pulpit ministry reached even to London, and several churches there tried to secure his service. But he loved his people at Trinity Church in Chester, and refused each invitation.

Matthew was usually in his study before five o'clock each morning, devoting himself to the preparation of his exposition of the Word. He had breakfast with his family and always led them in worship, reading and expounding some passage from the Old Testament. He then returned to his study until afternoon, when he would set out to visit his people. After the evening meal, he would again lead the household in worship, using a New Testament passage for his meditation. He often questioned the children and the servants to make sure they had understood the teaching.

Often in the late evening, he would put in a few more hours of study before retiring. "Take heed of growing remiss in your work," he warned fellow pastors. "Take pains while you live. . . . The Scripture still affords new things, to those who search them." It was not unusual for him to preach seven times a week, and yet he was always fresh and practical. "No place is like my own study," he said. "No company like good books, especially the book of God." We wonder what Matthew Henry would think of those ministers who rush about all week, wasting time, and then "borrow" another man's sermon for the Lord's Day.

The key date in Matthew Henry's life is November 12, 1704; on that day he started writing his famous *Commentary*. On April 17, 1714, he completed his comments on the Book of Acts; but two months later, on June 22, he suddenly took ill and died.

Matthew Henry was not pastoring in Chester when he was called home. On May 18, 1712, he had begun his new ministry in Hackney, London. One of the factors motivating his move was his desire to be closer to his publisher as his *Commentary* was being printed. He had ministered twenty-five years at Trinity Church, Chester, and only two years in London. The funeral service was held on June 25, and he was buried at Trinity Church.

Much of the material in Henry's *Commentary* came from his own expositions of Scripture given at family worship and from the pulpit. There is also a great deal of Philip Henry in these pages, especially the pithy sayings that season the exposition. Matthew's purpose in writing the *Commentary* was practical, not academic. He simply wanted to explain and apply the Word of God in language the common people could understand.

Several of his pastor friends gathered up his notes and sermons and completed the *Commentary* from Romans to

Revelation. When you read their expositions, you can see how far short they fall of the high standard set by the original author. In true Puritan fashion, Matthew Henry had the ability to get to the heart of a passage, outline the passage clearly, and then apply its truths to daily life. True, there were times when he spiritualized the text and missed the point; but generally speaking, he did his work well. One does not have to agree with all of his interpretations to benefit from his observations.

In 1765, John Wesley published an edited version of the *Commentary*, hoping to bring it within the reach of the average Christian reader. He felt the current version was too large and too expensive. But, at the same time, Wesley also deleted all that Matthew Henry had to say about election and predestination. He also omitted an "abundance of quaint sayings" and thus took the seasoning out of the dinner. In his preface, Wesley remarked that he used to wonder where some preachers "whom I greatly esteem" obtained the "pretty turns in preaching" that he heard in their sermons; but, after reading Matthew Henry, he discovered their source. I have a suspicion that this was a gentle criticism of his estranged friend, George Whitefield, who used to read Matthew Henry before going into the pulpit.

You will not find Matthew Henry grappling with big problems as he expounds the Word, or always shedding light on difficult passages in the Bible. For this kind of help you must consult the critical commentaries. He did not know a great deal about customs in the Holy Land, since travel to the East was quite limited in that day. Again, the student will need up-to-date commentaries and Bible dictionaries to help him in that area. However, for a devotional and practical approach to Bible exposition, this commentary leads the way.

I must confess that I have not followed Spurgeon's advice to read straight through *Matthew Henry's Commentary*, but I have used it with profit over the years. I think Henry is especially good in Genesis, Psalms, and the four Gospels. I have never consulted his *Commentary* early in my sermon preparation, but rather have left him (and Maclaren and Spurgeon) until after I had done my own digging and meditating. Often just a sentence from Matthew Henry has opened up a new area of thought for me and helped me feed my people.

I was surprised to discover that Matthew Henry is quoted in our two leading books of quotations. *Bartlett's Familiar Quotations* has fourteen Henry quotations and *The Oxford Dictionary of Quotations* (3rd edition) has six. Apparently Matthew Henry is the originator of the phrase "creature comforts" as well as the popular saying "All this and heaven too." Perhaps some enterprising reader could mine some of Matthew Henry's pithy sayings and put them into a book for us.

If you want to get to know this expositor and his father better, secure *The Lives of Philip and Matthew Henry*, published by Banner of Truth. Matthew Henry wrote the biography of his father, and it is a classic. J. B. Williams wrote the son's life, but it is not as exciting.

When he was on his deathbed, Matthew Henry said to a friend, "You have been asked to take notice of the sayings of dying men—this is mine: that a life spent in the service of God and communion with Him is the most pleasant life that anyone can live in this world."

2

Jonathan Edwards
1703–1758

It is unfortunate that many people imagine Jonathan Edwards as a ranting Puritan preacher, pounding the pulpit and trying to frighten sinners into heaven. Of course, most of these people have probably never read his famous sermon "Sinners in the Hands of an Angry God" or even examined the life of this godly man. For Jonathan Edwards was a quiet scholar, a loving father, a concerned pastor, a burdened missionary, and a man who loved God and longed more than anything else to glorify him.

Edwards was born into the home of Reverend Timothy Edwards in East Windsor, Connecticut, on October 5, 1703. He was the only son in the family; he had ten sisters. He came from good Puritan stock, especially on his mother's side of the family. Her father was Reverend Solomon Stoddard, revered pastor of the Congregational Church at Northampton, Massachusetts.

Stoddard was the accepted spiritual leader of the churches in the Connecticut Valley; in fact, some people called him "Pope" Stoddard. He pastored there for fifty years, and under his ministry at least five special spiritual awakenings had been experienced.

Jonathan Edwards received his schooling at home; at an early age he learned Latin, and later he took on Greek and Hebrew. He had two passionate interests in those early years—science and religion. He watched spiders and wrote an amazing essay about them. He saw the mind and heart of God in creation; everything in nature revealed to him something about God.

But his interest in spiritual things was remarkable for a boy so young. He prayed five times each day. With some of his friends he built a "booth" in the swamp, and there they would gather together to discuss spiritual matters and pray. I must confess that the boys' clubs my friends and I formed in our youthful years centered more around fun and games.

In 1716, when he was thirteen, Edwards entered Yale college, where he invested four years in undergraduate study and then two more years studying theology. It was while he was at Yale that he had two life-changing experiences. The first was his conversion when he was about seventeen years old. Since childhood he had revolted against the doctrine of the sovereignty of God. But as he read 1 Timothy 1:17, he had a remarkable experience of the sense of God's greatness and glory, and all his theological objections disappeared.

16

"As I read the words," he wrote in his personal account, "there came into my soul, and was as it were diffused through it, a sense of the glory of the divine Being; a new sense, quite different from anything I ever experienced before. . . . From about that time, I began to have a new kind of apprehensions and ideas of Christ, and the work of redemption, and the glorious way of salvation by Him."

Edwards was never content to have only book knowledge of God. He sought to experience God in his own life in a personal way. He was not an ivory-tower theologian, spinning webs of words. He always centered on the experience of the heart; it was this conviction that brought him many spiritual blessings as well as many spiritual battles.

His second crisis experience was more intellectual than spiritual, although Edwards would never divorce the mind and the heart. He read John Locke's *Essay Concerning Human Understanding* and made an about-face in his approach to the problem of how people think and learn. He came to the conclusion that "knowledge" was not something divorced from the rest of life, but that a man's senses helped to teach him truth. In other words, sensory experience and thinking must go together. Again, Edwards saw the importance of uniting the mind and the heart.

This approach would govern his philosophy of preaching for the rest of his life. He would first aim for the heart and move the affections before trying to instruct the mind. In one of his most important books, *A Treatise Concerning Religious Affections*, Edwards wrote, "True religion, in great part, consists in holy affections."[1] However, he opposed emotion for emotion's sake. He carefully explained the difference between shallow emotionalism and true affections that prepare the way for men and women to receive God's truth.

On January 12, 1723, Jonathan Edwards solemnly dedicated himself to God. Earlier he had made a list of resolutions that he read once each week and sought to obey daily. From time to time, he added to this list as he saw special needs in his life. He used it not as a law to bind him, but as a compass to guide him and as a mirror to help him examine his progress in his spiritual walk.

On February 15, 1727, Jonathan Edwards was ordained and became assistant to his grandfather, Solomon Stoddard. On July 20 of that same year, he married Sarah Pierrepont, an exemplary Christian lady who bore him eleven children. It is worth noting that Jonathan Edwards used to spend at least one hour each evening with his children before they went to bed. He often studied thirteen hours a day, yet he took time for his family. He and his wife were very happy together; their marriage and their home were a testimony to the goodness and grace of God.

In February 1729, Solomon Stoddard died, and Jonathan Edwards became the pastor of his church, perhaps the most important congregation outside Boston. Spiritual life in the American colonies was very low, and there was a desperate need for revival. Preachers were generally well-educated, but they lacked a burden for souls and power in preaching. Some of them were not even converted themselves!

"I am greatly persuaded," wrote George Whitefield when he visited New England, "that the generality of preachers talk of an unknown, unfelt Christ. And the reason why congregations have been so dead is because dead men preach to them."

But the preachers were not the only ones to blame. While the founders of the churches had, for the most part, been converted people who feared God, their children and grandchildren were too often unconverted but baptized church members.

The churches operated under what was known as the Half-Way Covenant. This permitted people to unite with the church if they had been baptized but had not made a profession of faith in Christ (they were baptized as infants, of course). Their children were then baptized as "half-way members," but they were not permitted to share the Lord's Supper or vote in church elections.

But Solomon Stoddard had gone even further in opening the doors of the church to unsaved people. He decided that the Lord's Supper was a saving ordinance and that unconverted people should not be barred from the table. The result, of course, was a church composed largely of unconverted people who gave lip service to the doctrine but who had never experienced the life of God in their own hearts.

Obviously, the new pastor and his flock were on a collision course. Edwards had experienced eternal life in an overwhelmingly personal way. It was his conviction that truth must be experienced in the heart as well as understood in the mind. In his study of the Word, he concluded that church membership and the Lord's Supper were for saved people alone. He realized that many of the "children of the covenant" in the colonies were living in sin, apart from God, and destined for eternal destruction.

In 1734 he preached a series of sermons on justification by faith. The time was ripe, and the Spirit began to move. In the next year, Edwards saw more than three hundred people unite with the church. Some notable sinners in the town were converted, and some remarkable events took place. This was one of the early phases of the spiritual movement in America historians call the Great Awakening, which covered a period from about 1725 to 1760.

Whenever the Spirit works, the flesh and the devil start to work to counterfeit God's blessing; and it was not long before excesses appeared in the revival movement. George Whitefield had joined the movement in 1740, and in some of his meetings people fainted, cried out with fear, and even experienced fits of shaking. Whitefield, like Edwards, did not encourage these activities, but had no control over them. Ministers who opposed religious enthusiasm openly criticized Edwards and accused him of leading the people astray, so Edwards wrote and published a book on how to discern a true working of God's Spirit: *The Distinguishing Marks of a Work of the Spirit of God*. It is still today one of the best studies of religious psychology available.

That same year (1741), Edwards was invited to preach at Enfield, Connecticut, and on July 8, he preached "Sinners in the Hands of an Angry God," perhaps the most famous sermon ever preached in America.

The text was Deuteronomy 32:35: "Their foot shall slide in due time." There is no question that Edwards had one purpose in mind: to shake the people out of their religious complacency and into the saving arms of the Lord. Edwards was always quiet in his delivery; he read from a manuscript and rarely looked at the people. He did not pound the pulpit or shout. He simply opened up the Scriptures and warned lost sinners to flee from the wrath to come.

The Spirit of God broke into the meeting, and many people came under conviction. Some cried out in fear. A minister sitting on the platform pulled at the preacher's coat-tails and said, "Mr. Edwards! Mr. Edwards! Is not God also a God of mercy!" Edwards had to stop preaching and wait for the congregation to become quiet. He concluded the sermon, led in prayer, and closed the meeting. Those who remained afterward to talk to the preacher were not necessarily upset or afraid. In fact, people were impressed with the cheerfulness and pleasantness of the expressions on others' faces.

Concerned with the salvation of the lost, Jonathan Edwards could not continue to live with the compromising situation that he had inherited at Northampton. In 1748, he informed the church that he would not receive as new members persons who had not given evidence of salvation, nor would he permit unconverted people to come to the Lord's table. Even though ministers in that day had far more authority and respect than they do today, this step was daring and was violently opposed by most of the other church leaders.

There followed nearly two years of debate and discussion, and the result was the dismissal of the pastor. Edwards preached his farewell sermon on July 1, 1750, a pastoral message that showed no animosity or bitterness, although certainly the preacher was a man with a broken heart. His text was 2 Corinthians 1:14, and his emphasis was on what would happen when ministers meet their congregations at the future judgment.

History has proven that Edwards was right and his congregation wrong. The colonial churches that rejected the working of God and refused to examine people as to their spiritual experience eventually turned from the faith and became liberal. The churches that followed Whitefield and Edwards continued to win the lost, send out missionaries, and train ministers who were true to the faith. An unconverted ministry and an unconverted membership are the devil's chief weapons in opposing the work of God.

Jonathan Edwards moved his wife and large family to Stockbridge, Massachusetts, where he ministered as a missionary to the Indians. His income was reduced, of course, and yet God provided all their needs. Freed from pastoral duties and church problems, Edwards now had more time to study and write; during those Stockbridge years (1751–58) he wrote several of his most important works, some of which were published after his death. In 1757 he was named president of Princeton College, an office that his son-in-law Aaron Burr later held. He took office in 1758 when a smallpox epidemic was invading the area; he caught the infection through an inoculation that backfired, and on March 22 he died.

We have had more than two hundred years to evaluate the life and ministry of Jonathan Edwards. He was perhaps the greatest thinker that America ever produced, and yet he had the heart of a child. He was a great theologian, and yet his books and sermons touch life and reach into the heart. He was a rare blend of biblical scholar and revivalist. He had a longing to see people know God personally, but he refused to accommodate his theology just to get results. He was also a man concerned about missions. Even the *Encyclopedia Britannica* admits, "By his writings and example, he gave impetus to the infant evangelical missionary movement."

Edwards was not afraid to give his people solid doctrine. His Resolution 28 reads: "Resolved to study the Scriptures so steadily, constantly, and frequently, so that I may find, and plainly perceive myself to grow in the knowledge of the same." Some preachers today seem to have time for everything else but Bible study and the preparation of spiritual nourishment for their people. It is easy to borrow a sermon from a book or listen to a recording of another preacher's message.

Edwards used imagination in his preaching. Like every good teacher and preacher, he turned the ear into an eye and helped people to *see* spiritual truth. He knew that the mind is not a debating chamber—it is a picture gallery.

He was a courageous man who held to his biblical convictions even though they cost him his church and the loss of many friends. He stood with George Whitefield when many were opposing him. Edwards encouraged spiritual awakening even though he knew there would be excesses and abuses. He would have enjoyed Billy Sunday's reply to the critic who said that revivals did not last: "Neither does a bath," said Sunday, "but it's good to have one once in a while!" Edwards preached for decisions in an era when ministers were not supposed to disturb the congregation.

The Works of President Edwards, a single volume, may be available in your local library. Ola Elizabeth Winslow has written one of the best biographies, *Jonathan Edwards*, published by Macmillan in 1940. She also edited a helpful anthology of his most important sermons and writings, *Jonathan Edwards: Basic Writings* (New American Library).

Jonathan Edwards on Heaven and Hell by Dr. John Gerstner (Baker Books) is a fascinating and very readable study of this important subject. Dr. Gerstner is perhaps our leading evangelical scholar when it comes to the life and theology of Jonathan Edwards. For a satisfying but readable study of Edwards's theology, read *Jonathan Edwards, Theologian of the Heart*, by Harold Simonson (Eerdmans).

Our nation is desperately in need of spiritual awakening. But our emphasis on evangelism apart from doctrine will certainly not do it. The Great Awakening was the result of solid doctrinal preaching that addressed itself to both the heart and the mind. It was preaching that dared to expose sin in the church. And God used it to sweep thousands into his family.

Perhaps it is time that we dug again these old wells and learned why their waters flowed with life so fruitfully and so bountifully.

3

John Henry Newman
1801–1890

If people today think at all of John Henry Newman, it is probably as the author of the familiar hymn "Lead, Kindly Light." Those who are somewhat acquainted with church history will identify him as one of the leaders of the Oxford Movement, which shook the Church of England and eventually led Newman himself into the Church of Rome. But it is Newman the preacher I want to examine in this chapter, the man whom W. Robertson Nicoll called "the most influential preacher Oxford has ever known,"[1] and whom Alexander Whyte admired so much that he wrote *Newman: An Appreciation*.

Newman was born in London on February 21, 1801. His family would be identified with the moderate evangelicals in the Church of England. At age fifteen, Newman experienced conversion. He was educated at Trinity College, Oxford, where he fell under the influence of Richard Whately. "He, emphatically, opened my mind, and taught me to think and to use my reason," Newman later wrote in his famous autobiography, *Apologia pro vita sua*. This was probably the beginning of Newman's drift from the evangelical emphasis and into the High Church party, and eventually to the Church of Rome.

However, it was his dear friend Richard Hurrell Froude who influenced Newman the most. "He taught me to look with admiration towards the Church of Rome," Newman wrote, "and in the same degree to dislike the Reformation." Froude did more than this: he introduced Newman to John Keble—brilliant Oxford scholar, humble Anglican pastor, and a man utterly devoted to the Church of England. Keble is remembered today as the writer of "Sun of My Soul, Thou Savior Dear," taken from his once-popular book of religious poetry, *The Christian Year*.

In 1824 Newman was ordained, and in 1828 he began his ministry as vicar of St. Mary's, Oxford. I can never forget stepping into that historic church one summer day and actually climbing the stairs into Newman's pulpit. As I stood there, I could hear faintly the Oxford traffic outside; but I quickly found myself carried, via imagination, to a Sunday afternoon service at which Newman was preaching. The church was filled with worshipers, mostly the younger fellows of the colleges and the undergraduates. Newman came in—"gliding" is the way one observer described it—and made his way to the pulpit, where he adjusted the gas lamp, laid his manuscript before him, and then in a musical voice that haunted, began to preach in a way that penetrated one's very being. "It was from the pulpit of St. Mary's that he began to conquer and to rule the world," wrote Alexander Whyte, one of Newman's most ardent Protestant admirers.

The rest of the story need not delay us. On July 14, 1833, Keble preached the "assize sermon" at St. Mary's, and his theme was "national apostasy." It was this sermon that gave birth to the concern that eventuated in what we know as the Oxford Movement (not to be confused with the Oxford Group Movement begun by Frank Buchman and later re-named Moral Re-armament). The burden of the movement was spiritual renewal in the Church of England. Newman, Keble, Froude, E. B. Pusey, and their associates sought to restore the spiritual authority of the church and to return the church to its ancient moorings. Their motives were commend-able; their methods perhaps left something to be desired.

One of their chief ministries was the publication of "tracts for the times." Various men—not all as gifted as Newman—wrote on subjects pertaining to the Church of England. The critics noticed a Rome-ward trend in the tracts, but the writ-ers persisted. It was *Tract Ninety* that wrote *finis* to Newman's leadership in the movement and his ministry at St. Mary's. In this famous pamphlet, Newman tried to prove that the Thirty-nine Articles of the Church of England could be honestly interpreted from a Roman Catholic point of view. The result was official censure—the politics of the controversies from 1833 to 1845 are worthy of study—and Newman could do nothing but either step aside or recant. Deeply hurt by the church leaders he had thought would encourage him, New-man left Oxford; and on October 8, 1845, he was received into the Roman Catholic church.

I find the history of the Oxford Movement fascinating. In it one finds events and leaders that parallel situations we have today. There is really nothing new under the sun. People today who want to "purify" or "renew" the church would do well to read up on the Oxford Movement and then avoid its mistakes. *The Oxford Movement* by R. W. Church, dean of St. Paul's, is the best introduction. A more modern study is *The Oxford Conspirators* by Marvin R. O'Connell. It is desirable to read Newman's own account in *Apologia pro vita sua*, and keep in mind that he wrote this some twenty years after these events.

But now to Newman's preaching.

Between 1824, when he was ordained, and 1845, when he left Oxford, Newman preached over one thousand sermons, ten volumes of which are available today. His eight volumes of *Parochial and Plain Sermons* represent the best of his pulpit ministry at St. Mary's. *Sermons Bearing on Subjects of the Day* and *Fifteen Sermons Preached Before the University of Oxford* are two volumes that complete the Protestant years. *Discourses Addressed to Mixed Congregations* and *Sermons Preached on Various Occasions* come from his Roman Catholic years.

I was amazed when I learned that Whyte had been such an admirer of Newman; for if any preacher emphasized the grace of God and the gospel of Jesus Christ, it was Whyte. Yet Whyte told a friend that he valued Newman's sermons more than those of F. W. Robertson! On March 14, 1876, Whyte and some friends visited Newman at the oratory in Edgbaston and were received graciously. Whyte even incorporated in his *Catechism* a revision from Newman that clarified the doctrine of transubstantiation. There is no escaping the fact that Alexander Whyte admired John Henry Cardinal Newman.

Let us begin with the obvious reason: Newman's sermons, not unlike Whyte's, were directed to the conscience. "The effect of Newman's preaching on us young men," wrote William Lockhart, "was to turn our souls inside out!" In this, Whyte was a kindred spirit of Newman, for few evangelical preachers can expose sin and "perform spiritual surgery" like Alexander Whyte! But another factor was Newman's "otherworldliness." He, like Whyte, had an utter disdain of earthly things. Whyte reveled among the mystics and constantly called his congregation to a life of reality in the things of the Spirit. While Whyte would point sinners to the Lamb of God, however, Newman would find this life of the Spirit in a sacramental system.

Newman's ability to examine a text and then develop it into a sermon was something Whyte greatly admired. "For, let any young man of real capacity once master Newman's methods of exposition, discussion, and argumentation; his way of addressing himself to the treatment of a subject; his way of entering upon a subject, worming his way to the very heart of it, working it out, and winding it up," wrote Whyte in his *Appreciation*, and that man would "soon make his presence and his power felt in any of our newspapers or magazines."[2]

Add to this Newman's pure English style—"the quiet perfection of his English style," wrote Whyte's biographer—and you can understand why the old Covenanter so much appreciated the preaching of Cardinal Newman.

Whyte was careful to point out his disagreements with Newman, not the least of which was Newman's neglect of preaching the good news of salvation through faith in Jesus Christ. When Newman's sermons are "looked at as pulpit work, as preaching the Gospel," wrote Whyte, "they are full of the most serious, and even fatal, defects. . . . They are not, properly speaking, New Testament preaching at all. . . . As an analysis of the heart of man, and as a penetrating criticism of human life, their equal is nowhere to be found. But, with all that, they lack the one all-essential element of all true preaching—the message to sinful man concerning the free grace of God. . . . Newman's preaching—and I say it with more pain than I can express—never once touches the true core, and real and innermost essence, of the Gospel."[3]

Why bother to read the sermons of a man who did not preach the gospel, a man who eventually preached himself right out of an evangelical tradition and into a sacramental system? Because Newman can help teach us how to preach to a man's conscience, how to get beneath the surface and apply spiritual truth where it is needed. Newman was a better diagnostician than a dispenser of healing medicine ("I never take down Newman's sermons for my recovery and my comfort," admitted Whyte); but it is easier to apply the medicine after you have convinced the patient of his need.

It is worth noting that Newman warned against magnifying preaching above the other ministries of the church. In this, I think, he was reacting against the tendency on the part of some evangelicals of the day to turn their preachers into celebrities. Newman believed strongly in the continuity of

30

the church and the need for sermons to minister to the body collectively. He himself shunned and even fled from becoming "a popular preacher," and he had little confidence in men who used the pulpit to promote themselves.

It is unfortunate that Newman did not know the better evangelical men of that day. He saw only (or perhaps only wanted to see) a ministry that emphasized correct doctrine and dedicated zeal, but lacked Christian character and true spiritual power. R. W. Church described evangelicals as people with "an exhausted teaching and a spent enthusiasm." The evangelical churches were "respectable" and popular with men of position, but (added Church) "they were on very easy terms with the world."[4] If there was one thing Newman hated with a holy zeal, it was a religion of words without reality, words that described an experience but failed to effect it in the lives of people.

Newman desired to elevate worship in the church. While I do not agree with his sacramentalism, I do applaud his purpose; it is my conviction that true worship is the greatest need in our churches today. How easy it is to have words without power (Paul was aware of this—read 1 Thess. 1:5) and program without substance, especially in an evangelical church. Newman would have agreed with William Temple's definition of *worship*: "to quicken the conscience by the holiness of God, to feed the mind with the truth of God, to purge the imagination by the beauty of God, to open up the heart to the love of God, to devote the will to the purpose of God." We do not experience this kind of worship in many churches today, and often the preacher is to blame. Newman spoke about the "rudeness, irreverence, and almost profaneness . . . involved in pulpit addresses, which speak of the adorable works and sufferings of Christ, with the familiarity and absence of awe with which we speak about our friends."

Next to irreverence and the "unreality of words," Newman abhorred preaching that tried to cover "three or four subjects at once." He insisted that each sermon have a definite purpose expressed in a concrete statement. "Definiteness is the life of preaching," he wrote in *Lectures and Essays on University Subjects*, "a definite hearer, not the whole world; a definite topic, not the whole evangelical tradition; and, in like manner, a definite speaker. Nothing that is anonymous will preach."[5] Of course, the ultimate aim of all preaching is the salvation of the hearer, but this can be accomplished only when the preacher is prepared and knows what his aim is. We preach to persuade, and we must preach to the emotions as well as to the intellect, always using simple and concrete language.

The thing that impresses me about Newman's sermons is their freshness of spiritual expression. He did not preach on the "topics of the day." He carefully explained some first principle of the Christian life, some doctrine of the Christian faith, and wedded it to the practical life of the worshiper. He shunned oratory and sought to make the message of the Word the most important thing and the messenger the least important. He did not even debate the great issues involved in the Oxford Movement. Rather he strengthened and extended the movement by avoiding the issues and dealing with the fundamental truths that gave rise to these issues.

There are men called by God to preach on the issues of the hour, and we need their ministry. But for permanent strengthening of the church, we also need preachers who will dig again the old wells and lead us intelligently down the old paths and who, renouncing cheap pulpit rhetoric, will focus the white light of revelation on the human heart and examine us in that light. In short, today we need preaching that appeals to the conscience, penetrating preaching, clinical preaching, preaching that moves men to cry, "Men and brethren, what shall we do?" Newman's preaching did this.

But let us go one step further: let us apply the blessed medicine of the gospel (something Newman did not do) and reply to those under conviction, "Believe on the Lord Jesus Christ, and you shall be saved!" Newman would run to the beaten man at the side of the road and pour in the wine; but he could not pour in the oil.

If you want to get acquainted with Cardinal Newman, start with *Newman: An Appreciation* by Whyte. Then secure *The Preaching of John Henry Newman*, edited by Newman scholar W. D. White. White's scholarly introduction will acquaint you with Newman's world and his philosophy of preaching. I think both Newman and White were too hard on the evangelicals, but this is a minor fault in an otherwise capable essay. White included thirteen sermons that Newman considered his best. If you are interested in owning more of Newman's sermons, visit your local Catholic bookshop or watch the used-book stores in your area.

The best modern biography of Newman is Meriol Trevor's two-volume *Newman*. The first volume is subtitled *The Pillar of the Cloud*, the second *Light in Winter.* The author has also abridged this work into a one-volume edition titled *Newman's Journey*.

Newman wrote materials other than sermons, some excellent and some not so good. *A Newman Reader*, edited by Francis X. Connolly, will give you a rich sampling of his writings. My favorite edition of his autobiography, *Apologia pro vita sua*, is the one edited by David J. DeLaura. It contains all the necessary texts of Newman's controversy with Charles Kingsley, plus helpful notes that clarify material in the text.

One final observation: When I read Newman's sermons, I find myself examining not only my heart but also my preaching. I find myself asking: Am I a faithful physician of the soul? Am I preaching to the conscience? Am I faithful to declare truth, not simply my "clever ideas" about truth? Do I offer Christ as the only Redeemer? Do I get beneath the surface and help my hearers where they need it most? While I disagree with Newman's theology, I appreciate his preaching and have learned from it.

4

J. B. Lightfoot
1828–1889

The English Revised Version of the New Testament was placed in the hands of the British people on May 17, 1881, culminating ten years of work by fifty-four outstanding scholars. Public response was predictable: this new version, with all its announced accuracy, could never replace the Authorized Version with its beauty and, above all, familiarity.

The Anglican clergy were confused: could they legally use the new version when only the old version was officially authorized by the church? The man in the street was critical and skeptical. After all, the translators had promised not to deviate too much from the King James Version, and yet they had made 36,000 changes. Perhaps the new version was more accurate, but the public preferred tradition to scholarship. Prime Minister William Gladstone stated the problem clearly: "You will sacrifice truth if you don't read it, and you will sacrifice the people if you do." But Charles H. Spurgeon put the finger on the real problem: "It is strong in Greek, weak in English."

Indeed the new version *was* "strong in Greek," and one reason was the presence on the New Testament Committee of the "Cambridge triumvirate"—B. F. Westcott, F. J. A. Hort, and J. B. Lightfoot—names that still stand for scholarship in New Testament studies. Of the three, Lightfoot was undoubtedly the best scholar. In fact, Owen Chadwick called Lightfoot "the greatest scholar in the Jerusalem Chamber."[1] In his memorial essay on Bishop Lightfoot, W. Robertson Nicoll called him "pre-eminently the scholar of the Church of England."[2]

If you have ever used Lightfoot's commentaries on Galatians, Philippians, and Colossians, or any of his studies on the church fathers, you probably agree with Nicoll's conclusion. But what you may not know is that Bishop Lightfoot was a godly man, a teacher of pastors, and a preacher with a burden for lost souls. "When goodness is joined to knowledge, it counts for much," wrote Nicoll, "and when these are crowned by spiritual power, paramount influence is the result. Lightfoot had all three."[3]

Joseph Barber Lightfoot was born in Liverpool on April 13, 1828. He was taught at King Edward's School, Birmingham, by the noted James Prince Lee, whose pupils seemed to capture every prize and move into places of influence, particularly in the church. Lee taught Lightfoot to love the Greek New Testament; and the teacher saw in the pupil tremendous potential for both Christian character and scholarship. "Give him the run of the town library!" Lee ordered.

At age nineteen, Lightfoot entered Trinity College, Cambridge, where he studied under Westcott. ("He was Westcott's best pupil," Hort later admitted.) He captured several honors and prizes and seemed destined for a teaching position. In 1854 he was ordained a deacon in the Church of England, and in 1858 he was ordained as a priest. The next year he became a tutor at Trinity College, and in 1861 was named Hulsean Professor of Divinity. So popular were his New Testament lectures that they had to be given in the college's great hall. Ten years later he was made canon of St. Paul's, sharing the ministry with the great Henry Liddon and Dean R. W. Church. He was named Lady Margaret Professor of Divinity in 1875, and it seemed that his ministry as scholar, writer, and teacher was established.

But in 1879 he was appointed bishop of Durham, and the scholar had to make the most critical decision of his life. In the last public message Bishop Lightfoot preached, on June 29, 1889, he confessed that he had spent a "long wakeful night" making the decision to leave Cambridge and a life of scholarship for Durham and a life of administration. He wrote to his friend Westcott:

> At length I have sent my answer "Yes." It seemed to me that to resist any longer would be to fight against God. My consolation and my hope for the future is that it has cost me the greatest moral effort, the greatest venture of faith which I ever made. Now that the answer is sent I intend to have no regrets about the past.

Westcott called the decision "a kind of martyrdom," and perhaps it was.

In the months that followed, Lightfoot received letters from all kinds of people urging him to continue his studies and writing in spite of his new ministry. In a memorial sermon to Lightfoot, given on November 24, 1929, George R. Eden said: "Few men can have passed through such an agony of choice as we know he suffered. . . . Yet the choice was made—upon his knees, 'wrestling with the Angel in prayer.'" It is interesting to note that R. W. Dale warned Westcott in 1883: "Forgive me for saying—do not let them make you a bishop. I do not know what Dr. Lightfoot may have done for Durham; for those of us who are outside he has done nothing since his elevation."

What did the great Greek scholar do for Durham and for the Church of England? His years as bishop are still called "the golden age of Durham."

Westcott preached the consecration sermon (April 25, 1879) and urged the new bishop to "choose between the im-portant and the routine . . . and do the important." Lightfoot did so gladly, delegating routine matters to his associates and concentrating on the things only a bishop could do. Lightfoot was gifted with the mental, physical, and spiritual equipment a man needs to make a success of such a high office. He had a robust constitution and a love of hard work. An early riser, he put in two or three hours of study before breakfast, and he often remained at his desk when the rest of the staff had gone to bed. He had a remarkable memory and could tell a secretary where a quotation was in a given book, even its location on the page.

During a holiday in Norway, he was seen correcting proofs while riding in a cart on a rather precipitous road. He was a gifted linguist, fluent in French, German, Spanish, Italian, and Latin, as well as Greek; he was able to use Hebrew, Syriac, Arabic, Coptic, Ethiopic, and Armenian. He enjoyed telling the story about the professor who isolated several newborn babies to discover what language they would speak if not influenced by English. After a pause, Lightfoot would say, "The poor little children spoke pure Hebrew."

The new bishop was a worker and an innovator, much to the surprise and delight of the clergy under his jurisdiction. One of his first innovations was the "Brotherhood." Never married, Lightfoot each year "adopted" several young men who studied with him for a year before their ordination. It was an internship program on the highest level. But the bishop made it clear to applicants that the fellowship was "a brotherhood in Christ, not an exclusive association of clique or caste," and that their union was based on "participation in a common work and the loving devotion to a common Master." The bishop was their leader, teacher, example, and spiritual father. As one member of the Brotherhood put it, "We read, we worked, because Lightfoot was working and reading."

Men in the Brotherhood—"the sons of the house," as the bishop called them—were kept busy. They breakfasted with Lightfoot at 7:45, at 8:15 were in the chapel for morning prayers, and by 9:00 were either reading or listening to lectures. They ate lunch at 1:15, then scattered for practical ministry in the diocese. Each man was assigned a district where he worked with resident clergy. The men gathered during the week to share experiences and learn from one another, always under the watchful eye of the bishop. As the program developed, Bishop Lightfoot set aside St. Peter's Day (June 29) for an annual reunion of the "sons of the house." (Spurgeon followed a similar pattern with the men in his Pastors' College.)

The bishop viewed the Christian ministry highly, and he applied high standards to himself before he applied them to others. His essay "The Christian Ministry" in his commentary on Philippians upset more than one Anglican, who saw it as a departure from Church of England tradition. His friend Canon Liddon requested him to withdraw the essay, but Lightfoot refused to do it. "The Christian minister, whatever else he is—and I shall not enter upon controversial questions—is, before all things, a pastor, a shepherd," said Lightfoot in his last public appearance in his diocese.

Bishop Lightfoot also blended scholarship and Christian devotion. I once listened to an impassioned sermon by a well-known preacher on the impossibility of being both "a soul-winner and a deep Bible student." The apostle Paul would have smiled at that sermon, as would Charles G. Finney, Jonathan Edwards, R. A. Torrey, Charles Spurgeon, and J. B. Lightfoot. All Greek students should write on the flyleaf of their Greek New Testament these words of Bishop Lightfoot: "After all is said and done, the only way to know the Greek Testament properly is by prayer."

Lightfoot's own walk with God was the secret power of his life, and his concern to obey God and help others find Christ motivated him. He reorganized his diocese so that pastors would be able to reach more people and build more new churches. A great admirer of John Wesley, Lightfoot organized lay evangelists who helped carry the message from district to district. He mobilized the women of the diocese and encouraged them to serve in "sisterhoods" or as deaconesses. Before long, Durham was vibrating with new power and excitement because a great Greek scholar had placed himself and his ambitions on the altar that he might serve God. What he said to the Brotherhood, he practiced himself: "You go where you are sent, you work till you drop."

Lightfoot is best remembered as a writer. His commentaries on Galatians, Philippians, Colossians, and Philemon ought to be in every pastor's library. These scholarly works are part of a series that he had projected with his friends Westcott and Hort. The series was not completed, but Westcott did publish excellent commentaries on the Gospel of John, Hebrews, and the Epistles of John. Lightfoot died before he could write his commentary on Ephesians to complete the quartet. Lightfoot also wrote four articles for *Smith's Dictionary of the Bible* (Acts, Romans, 1 Thess., and 2 Thess.) and published the definitive edition of *The Apostolic Fathers*. The latter work demolished the position of the Tübingen school that centered around F. C. Baur, the German critic. More of a historian than a theologian, Lightfoot was at home with ancient documents and textual problems.

When an anonymous author attacked his friend Westcott in *Supernatural Religion*, Lightfoot took up his pen and wrote a series of articles for the *Contemporary Review* that pushed the bestselling book off the market. His facts were so devastating that the public rejected *Supernatural Religion*, and the book ended up glutting the used-book stores. Lightfoot's book *On a Fresh Revision of the English New Testament* is still available, as are several posthumous collections: *Ordination Addresses, Leaders in the Northern Church, Cambridge Sermons, Sermons Preached on Special Occasions, Sermons Preached in St. Paul's,* and *Historical Essays.*

Lightfoot had requested that no official biography be written; however, a memoir, *Bishop Lightfoot,* was published anonymously in 1894. Hort wrote the excellent article on Lightfoot in *The Dictionary of National Biography;* in fact, it was the last thing Hort wrote before his death. *Lightfoot of Durham: Memories and Appreciations* was edited by George R. Eden and F. C. Macdonald, and published in 1933.

Westcott did not heed Dale's warning. Not only did he become a bishop, but he succeeded Lightfoot at Durham. And his successor was one of Lightfoot's students, Handley C. G. Moule, also a Greek scholar and writer of commentaries. Durham was privileged to have men who combined academic excellence with spiritual fervor, resulting in a balanced ministry.

The day after Bishop Lightfoot died, one of the leading British newspapers, the *Times,* said: "He was at once one of the greatest Theological scholars and an eminent Bishop. It is scarcely possible to estimate adequately as yet the influence of his life and work." In preparing his "sons" for ordination, Bishop Lightfoot used to say: "Forget me, forget the [ordination] service of tomorrow, forget the human questioner. Transport yourselves in thought from the initial to the final inquiry. The great day of inquisition, the supreme moment of revelation, is come. The chief Shepherd, the universal bishop of souls is the questioner. . . . The 'Wilt thou' of the ordination day is exchanged for the 'Hast thou' of the judgment day." This is good counsel for all of us, but especially for those who serve as ministers and who want to hear our Master say, "Well done."

5

J. Hudson Taylor
1832–1905

A Presbyterian moderator in a Melbourne, Australia, church used all his eloquence to introduce the visiting missionary speaker, finally presenting him to the congregation as "our illustrious guest." He was not prepared for James Hudson Taylor's first sentence: "Dear friends, I am the little servant of an illustrious Master."

Nearly twenty years before, Hudson Taylor had written in an editorial: "All God's giants have been weak men, who did great things for God because they reckoned on His being with them." As he looked at himself, Hudson Taylor saw nothing but weakness; but as generations of Christians have studied Taylor's life, they have become acquainted with a man who dared to believe the Word of God and, by faith, carried the gospel to inland China—and saw God work wonders! "Want of trust is at the root of almost all our sins and all our weaknesses," he wrote in that same editorial, "and how shall we escape it but by looking to Him and observing His faithfulness. The man who holds God's faithfulness will not be foolhardy or reckless, but he will be ready for every emergency."

How Hudson Taylor became a man of faith is a story that every Christian—and every Christian worker in particular—ought to know well, because in that story is the kind of spiritual encouragement that we need in these difficult days.

Begin by reading *Hudson Taylor's Spiritual Secret*, written by his son and daughter-in-law, Howard and Mary Taylor. It is available in several paperback editions, although a cloth edition may still be available from the Overseas Missionary Fellowship, formerly known as the China Inland Mission. You may want to read the book twice—it is not long or difficult—and then secure the one-volume biography of Taylor by the same authors. The China Inland Mission published a beautiful centennial edition in 1965, but it is difficult to secure now. Fortunately, Moody Press has reprinted it in paperback with the title *God's Man in China*. This one-volume biography is a careful abridgement of a definitive two-volume work—*Hudson Taylor in Early Years* and *Hudson Taylor and the China Inland Mission*. If I were teaching a pastoral theology course in a seminary, I would require my students to read these two books to discover how God builds a man and then uses that man to build a work. It is unfortunate that this set is now out of print. The abridgement gives us all the important material we need, but the larger work includes sidelights and details that delight any reader interested in living history.

James Hudson Taylor was born on May 21, 1832, in Barnsley, Yorkshire, England. Taylor's parents were godly people who had dedicated their firstborn to the Lord, for their heart's desire was that their son serve Christ. Even while still a child of four or five, Hudson Taylor showed a concern for the "heathen" in foreign lands. "When I am a man," he would tell visitors in the home, "I mean to be a missionary and go to China." His father was a chemist (American translation: druggist) by trade and was very active as a Methodist preacher in his district. Often the local pastors would gather at the Taylor table to discuss their work, and young Hudson would listen with keen interest. "I used to love to hear them talk," he recalled years later. "Theology, sermons, politics, the Lord's work at home and abroad, all were discussed with so much earnestness and intelligence. It made a great impression upon us as children."

He had just turned seventeen when he was converted, and a short time later he felt a call to Christian service. He had experienced most of the trials and temptations of youth, and the tugging of the Holy Spirit on his heart; but for some reason he had resisted the call of God. The story of his conversion has often been told, but it is one that gets more wonderful with each telling. His mother had left him home alone while she visited a friend nearly a hundred miles away. Impressed by the Spirit to pray for her son, she left the table, went to her room, locked the door, and prayed for hours until she sensed in her heart that young Hudson had trusted Christ. Back at home, Hudson had found a tract in his father's library and was reading it primarily for the interesting stories that it might contain. While he was reading, he was struck by the phrase "the finished work of Christ." Immediately the words of Scripture leaped into his mind: "It is finished!" He said to himself, "If the whole work was finished and the whole debt paid, what is there left for me to do?" He fell to his knees and yielded himself to Christ; and when his mother returned home two weeks later, she told him she already knew!

Most people forget that Taylor was trained in medicine, and it was during his student days that he learned to trust God for every need. He realized that he could not leave England for some foreign land if he had not learned to prove God at home. How he trusted God for finances, not only for himself but also for others; how he was miraculously spared after being infected in the dissecting room; and how he grew in his exercise of faith are all told in the biographies, and what exciting chapters they are! You feel as if you are revisiting the book of Acts.

At this point Taylor's life takes on special interest for the Christian worker, for it is easy to see that Taylor permitted God to prepare him for the work he was calling him to do. It is for this reason that his biographers have devoted an entire volume of over five hundred pages to these first twenty-eight years of his life, his years of preparation. They say in the introduction to *Hudson Taylor in Early Years*:

> At first sight it might appear to some that to devote not less than half of the biography of one who did a great deal of public work, to a description of his preparation for that work, evidences some lack of the sense of due proportion.

The authors were fully alive to this aspect of the subject; but as they studied and pondered over the materials at their disposal, it was impressed upon them, with growing force, that the experience and the career of Mr. Taylor furnished a notable illustration of the truth that when God raises up a man for special service He first works in that man the principles which later on are, through his labors and influence, to be the means of widespread blessing to the Church and to the world.[1]

We need this emphasis today. We have too many "celebrities" and not enough servants—"nine-day wonders" that may flash across the scene for a time and then disappear. Before God works *through* us, he works *in* us, because the work that we do is the outgrowth of the life that we live. Jesus spent thirty years preparing for three years of ministry! The statement may have become a cliché, but it is still true that "God prepares us for what he is preparing for us."

On September 19, 1853, Hudson Taylor sailed for China as a representative of the Chinese Evangelization Society; even on the ship he had opportunity to witness for Christ and to trust God for miracles. At one stage of the voyage the ship lost its wind and began to drift toward a dangerous reef. Taylor and three other Christians on board prayed earnestly for God's help, and after a brief time of prayer, Taylor was convinced in his heart that God had answered. He went on deck and suggested to the first officer ("a godless man") that he let down the mainsail and make ready for the wind. The man cursed and refused to act. At that point the corner of the topmost sail began to tremble, and Taylor urged the man to move quickly. Before long, a strong wind began to blow and the ship was on its way!

From the very outset of his ministry in China, Hudson Taylor preferred to work independently. He had no particular denominational connections, yet was friendly with all who professed to know Christ. (His own convictions were Baptist.) He did medical work but was not a doctor; he did pastoral work but was not ordained. His life of discipline and sacrifice distinguished him among the missionaries. This does not mean that he rejected those who worked in the traditional ways. It was just that he preferred an independent ministry that left him free to follow God's leading without consulting the plans of men. It was this kind of devotion to Christ that led him to resign from the Chinese Evangelization Society in June 1857. Eight years later, on June 27, 1865, he officially founded the China Inland Mission.

On January 20, 1858, Hudson Taylor married Maria J. Dyer in China, and their romance is a love story that no fiction writer could concoct! For a detailed account read *Hudson Taylor and Maria* by John Pollock. Pollock claimed that the official biography errs in the order of events relating to Hudson's courting of Miss Dyer, suggesting that the missionary's memory failed him when he told his daughter-in-law the story years later.[2]

But the real bombshell in the Pollock book is his claim that in 1869, during the darkest hours of the mission, Hudson Taylor was so discouraged that he was tempted to end his own life! "Maria stood between Hudson and suicide," stated Pollock.[3] I once asked a veteran CIM missionary about this, and he claimed it was probably a misunderstanding. Pollock's source, he added, is "an unpublished note in the Taylor papers." Even if Hudson Taylor *did* express this kind of despair, two things are true: greater men than he have done the same (Moses and Elijah, for example); and he expressed it only *before* he experienced "the exchanged life." In fact, it was the valley experience of the Yanchow riots that prepared the way for his life-changing meeting with Christ.

There is no need for me to retell the story; you have it in *Hudson Taylor's Spiritual Secret*. On Saturday, September 4, 1869, Taylor read in a letter from missionary John McCarthy about the new freedom that had come into McCarthy's life. "Not a striving to have faith," McCarthy wrote, "but a looking off to the Faithful One seems all we need; a resting in the Loved One entirely, for time and for eternity." "As I read," said Taylor, "I saw it all. I looked to Jesus, and when I saw—oh, how joy flowed!" The "theology of the deeper life" is disturbing to some people, and for this reason they avoid it; but for Hudson Taylor "the exchanged life" was as simple and as real as salvation itself. His associates noticed the difference: he had a new power in ministry and a new poise in facing the problems of the mission. "He cast everything on God in a new way, and gave more time to prayer," wrote one co-laborer. "Instead of working late at night, he began to go to bed earlier, rising at 5:00 to give time to Bible study and prayer." I cannot urge you enough to read the whole story for yourself and then take it to heart.

One of the byproducts of reading Taylor's life is the introduction you receive to so many well-known Christians who, in one way or another, played a part in his life and ministry. For instance, D. L. Moody was on the platform when, in 1872, Taylor gave the opening address at the "Mildmay" conference for the deeper life.

The Student Volunteer Movement that grew out of Moody's Northfield ministry attracted Taylor tremendously. When he came to America in 1888, Taylor spoke at Northfield and Moody had to arrange extra meetings to allow the students to get the most out of Taylor's ministry. Of course the story of "the Cambridge seven" had reached North America, and it is possible that the dedication of these young men was one of the seeds that helped to bring the Student Volunteer Movement into fruition. There is little question that Moody's ministry in England assisted the progress of foreign missions in a tremendous way, and the China Inland Mission profited from this.

Moody and Taylor, of course, would disagree on the matter of financing the Lord's work. Both of them believed in prayer and trusting God, but Taylor refrained from asking anybody for support. "When our work becomes a begging work, it dies," said Taylor. Moody, on the other hand, was bold in asking Christians for financial support and raised huge sums for Christian enterprises both in the United States and Great Britain. While he greatly admired men like Hudson Taylor and George Müller, Moody felt that his own ministries operated by faith just as much as did theirs. He also felt that, sincere as they were, their emphasis on "making no appeals" was in itself an appeal. Thank God for the variety of men He uses, and thank God for men who can disagree without being disagreeable!

You also will meet other evangelical notables as you read the life of Hudson Taylor: F. B. Meyer (who was deeply moved by the Cambridge seven); H. Grattan Guinness, the British evangelist and Bible teacher (his daughter Mary Geraldine married Hudson Taylor's son, Howard, and helped him write the biography); Howard Kelly; W. J. Erdman; and many others. I was interested to discover that the founder of the Scandinavian Alliance Mission, Fredrik Franson, was greatly influenced by both Moody and Taylor. Taylor's pamphlet *To Every Creature* stirred this Swedish evangelist to form the Swedish Alliance Mission.

Taylor's principles of ministry may not be agreeable to everybody, but they are certainly worth considering. He is the originator, as far as I know, of the oft-quoted statement "God's work done in God's way will never lack God's supplies."[1] "And what does going into debt really mean?" he asked. "It means that God has not supplied your need. . . . If we can only wait *right up to the time*, God cannot lie, God cannot forget: He is *pledged* to supply all our need."[5] It was also a principle of his to promote *missions* and not simply the work of his mission alone. "We do not need to say much about the CIM," he wrote. "Let people see God working, let God be glorified, let believers be made holier, happier, brought nearer to Him and they will not need to be asked to help."[6] In this day when too many men and their ministries are glorified and when some Christian enterprises have been fiscally irresponsible, perhaps Hudson Taylor's counsel is appropriate. His word about trials is also needed: "We might be lifted up, perhaps, or lose spiritual life and power, if success were unaccompanied by discipline."[7]

After you have become acquainted with James Hudson Taylor through the books written *about* him, start reading the books written *by* him. The Moody Colportage series used to carry *Union and Communion*, Taylor's devotional commentary on the Song of Solomon (written while he was courting Maria!) and *A Retrospect*, his personal recollections. In 1931, the China Inland Mission published *Hudson Taylor's Legacy*, a series of devotional messages taken from Taylor's various articles and editorials originally published in the mission's magazine. This book was edited by Marshall Broomhall, whose ancestors were a part of the CIM ministry from the beginning. The book is especially valuable in that it presents, in his own words, Taylor's basic philosophy of missions and ministry. These three books are worth adding to your library.

One of Taylor's close associates, J. W. Stevenson, wrote of him, "Oh, his was a life that stood looking into!" I suggest you do more than "look into" his life. I suggest you get to know Hudson Taylor intimately; for when you do, if you are open at all to God's truth, the Holy Spirit will do something fresh and lasting in your heart. For the Christian seeking faith in troubled times, for the servant thirsting for fresh power, for the worker longing to know how to build for God, the life of James Hudson Taylor can point the way to Christ—the final answer to every need.

Taylor died on June 3, 1905, during his last visit to China, and he was buried in that land whose people he loved so dearly. But thanks to the printed page, "he being dead yet speaketh."

6

Charles H. Spurgeon
1834–1892

Perhaps one of the highest compliments anyone could pay a preacher would be to say that he preaches like Spurgeon. It would be nigh impossible to locate many people today who actually heard Charles H. Spurgeon preach (he died on January 31, 1892), but the compliment is valid just the same.

Spurgeon was a wonder in his own day, and he is still a wonder today. When the sermons of other men are covered with dust, Spurgeon's will still be read—and preached! But Spurgeon the man also needs to be discovered by each new generation of preachers, and perhaps rediscovered by some of us who first met him years ago. "Sell all that you have ... and buy Spurgeon!" wrote Helmut Thielicke in his *Encounter with Spurgeon*, and with this counsel we heartily agree.

Charles Haddon Spurgeon was a many-sided individual. You find his name appearing in almost every book that touches upon the religious scene in Victorian England. Just think of the years spanned by his ministry. In the year he was called to New Park Street Chapel, the Crimean War began. The year he opened the great Metropolitan Tabernacle, the United States Civil War began. While he was ministering, Karl Marx wrote his *The Communist Manifesto* and Charles Darwin his *Origin of Species.* He was contemporary with Phillips Brooks, Alexander Whyte, D. L. Moody, F. B. Meyer, Alexander Maclaren, R. W. Dale (whose theology he criticized), and Joseph Parker. To get acquainted with Spurgeon is to become familiar with one of the greatest eras of preaching in the history of the church.

I suggest you begin with *C. H. Spurgeon* by W. Y. Fullerton. Published in 1920, this book has the value of having been written by one who was close to the great preacher. In fact, from 1879 to 1893 Fullerton served as one of Spurgeon's assistants at the tabernacle, and often preached when he was away. For several years Fullerton edited Spurgeon's sermons for publication each week and became so imbued with the great preacher's style that it is almost impossible to detect where Spurgeon leaves off and his assistant begins! While Fullerton naturally wrote with great admiration for Spurgeon, this did not prevent Fullerton from gently disagreeing with his hero. It is a delightful, informative, and even an inspiring book; it bears reading and rereading. His final paragraph is a masterpiece: "To me he is master and friend. I have neither known nor heard of any other, in my time, so many-sided, so commanding, so simple, so humble, so selfless, so entirely Christ's man. Proudly I stand at the salute!"

Now that you have the broad landscape of Spurgeon before you, you can obtain his autobiography, published by Banner of Truth in two volumes entitled *Spurgeon*. The original autobiography was published serially between 1897 and 1900 and was compiled from his letters and records by his wife and private secretary. These four volumes are not easy to secure, so we are grateful for this new two-volume edition. It is not identical to the original autobiography in that some extraneous material has been omitted—primarily sermon outlines, newspaper quotations, and unimportant letters. But in two respects the new edition is superior: the editors have rearranged some sections to give greater continuity, and have added helpful footnotes. The beautiful thing about these two large volumes of more than one thousand pages is this: you can read a chapter at a sitting and, before you know it, complete the book! They are perfect to keep on your bedside table or near your favorite easy chair. Spurgeon wrote just as he preached—in clear Anglo-Saxon English—and his latest editors have not tried to improve upon his style.

It may shock you to discover that Spurgeon was not only a preacher; he was a fighter! He boldly preached the truth as he saw it in Scripture, and if his sermons hurt some individual or groups, he did not apologize. "Some things are true and some things are false—I regard that as an axiom," he said in one of his famous lectures to his students. "But there are many persons who evidently do not believe it. . . . We have a fixed faith to preach, my brethren, and we are sent forth with a definite message from God." However, he warned his young students, "Don't go about the world with your fist doubled up for fighting, carrying a theological revolver in the leg of your trousers." He practiced what he preached, but when his preaching did lead to controversy, he was not one to retreat. The best study of this aspect of Spurgeon's ministry is *The Forgotten Spurgeon*, written by Iain Murray. In nine carefully documented chapters, the author takes us through Spurgeon's battles over baptismal regeneration, Arminianism, and liberalism in the Baptist Union.

Spurgeon preached no diluted gospel, and when he heard other men preach that way, he heard a call to arms. His first declaration of war came shortly after he began publishing his weekly sermons in 1855. His Calvinistic theology upset some of the brethren: he was not Calvinistic enough for one group and he was too Calvinistic for another. The controversy raged in the pages of religious publications, with some writers even questioning Spurgeon's conversion! "I am not very easily put down," Spurgeon wrote to a friend. "I go right on and care for no man on God's earth."

The second controversy grew out of the sermon against baptismal regeneration, which was preached at the tabernacle on June 5, 1864.[1] His text was Mark 16:15–16. Spurgeon was sure that the message would completely destroy the ministry of his printed sermons, but just the opposite occurred. His publishers sold over a quarter of a million copies! Fullerton stated that a "blizzard of pamphlets and sermons" swept down upon the churches as a result of this one message and that Spurgeon seemed to enjoy it!

"I hear you are in hot water," a friend said to him.

"Oh, no," Spurgeon replied. "It is the other fellows who are in hot water. I am the stoker, the man who makes the water boil."

Of course Spurgeon was aiming at something much larger than the doctrine of baptismal regeneration. He was concerned about the growing influence of Romanism in England, and he was bold to say so. This was the Puritan in Spurgeon, fighting for biblical truth and making any sacrifice necessary to defend the doctrines of God's grace.

Spurgeon's third controversy was perhaps the most painful for him because it touched the fellowship of the brethren in the Baptist Union. In 1887 he published, in his *Sword and Trowel* magazine, several articles dealing with the growing heresy in Baptist churches. The first two articles were called "The Down-Grade," and this led to the popular identification of the battle as the "down-grade controversy." "It now becomes a serious question," Spurgeon wrote, "how far those who abide by the faith once delivered to the saints should fraternize with those who have turned aside to another gospel. Christian love has its claims, and divisions are to be shunned as grievous evils; but how far are we justified in being in confederacy with those who are departing from the truth?" On October 28, 1887 (Fullerton said October 8, but this is an error), Spurgeon withdrew from the Baptist Union.[2] "Fellowship with known and vital error is participation in sin," he wrote in the November *Sword and Trowel*. His decision was final and it was public; now the Baptist Union had to act. What they did and how they did it is beautifully recorded in Murray's book, and it stands (in my opinion) as a sorry indictment of a group of men who should have known better. Fullerton believed that Spurgeon himself should have come to the Baptist Union assembly, but since he had already resigned, this would have been impossible.

Alexander Maclaren was one of four pastors assigned to meet with Spurgeon, but he kept himself completely out of the matter. We wonder why. After Spurgeon's death, the Baptist Union put in the entrance to its headquarters an imposing statue of Spurgeon!

But let's turn from these disappointing events and consider some other facets of this man's amazing life and ministry. It is well known that Spurgeon smoked, although it must be admitted that many famous British preachers smoked. (I have been told by one who ought to know that Campbell Morgan smoked as many as eight cigars a day! And R. W. Dale said that he could get along without food more easily than without his tobacco.) Once Spurgeon was gently reprimanded for his smoking by a Methodist preacher. "If I ever find myself smoking to excess, I promise I shall quit entirely," Spurgeon said.

"What would you call smoking to excess?" the man asked.

"Why, smoking two cigars at the same time!" was the answer.

In *Echoes and Memories*, Bramwell Booth's interesting book of reminiscences, this son of the founder of the Salvation Army mentioned Spurgeon's habit of smoking. Scheduled to preach at a Salvation Army meeting, Spurgeon arrived "in a fine carriage, smoking a cigar. His remark that he smoked to the honor and glory of God is one of those oft-quoted sayings which have done infinite harm to the world, putting into the mouth of many a youth not only a poisonous weed but a flippant and irreligious apology."[3]

Strange to say, while Spurgeon saw no harm in tobacco, he did oppose the theater. In fact, it was this (among other things) that precipitated his famous "open-letter" controversy with the famous Joseph Parker, eloquent pastor of the City Temple in London. Parker's congregation was second in size only to Spurgeon's, but his ecclesiastical circle was much wider and much more diversified. Spurgeon had been preaching in London for fifteen years when Parker came to Poultry Chapel (which later became the famous City Temple), and the men were on good terms. They exchanged pulpits and on occasion preached in support of various Christian enterprises in the city. On February 23, 1887, Parker invited Spurgeon to address an interdenominational gathering in defense of "the old evangelical faith." The next day Spurgeon wrote a letter of refusal, kindly pointing out that Parker's own ministry did not consistently defend the faith. The fuse had been lit. Parker immediately wanted to know if there was "aught against thy brother" and, if so, why Spurgeon had not told him sooner. Spurgeon replied, among other things: "The evangelical faith in which you and Mr. Beecher agree is not the faith which I hold; and the view of religion which takes you to the theater is so far off from mine that I cannot commune with you therein." Parker's reply was on a postcard: "Best thanks, and best regards—J. P."[4]

The matter was forgotten until April 25, 1890, when Parker published an open letter to Spurgeon in the influential *British*

Weekly, edited by W. Robertson Nicoll. Spurgeon's Pastors' College Conference was in session that week, making Parker's attack that much more devastating. Nicoll himself was a great admirer and defender of Spurgeon, and it is difficult to understand why he published the letter. It said in part:

> Let me advise you to widen the circle of which you are the center. You are surrounded by offerers of incense. They flatter your weakness, they laugh at your jokes, they feed you with compliments. My dear Spurgeon, you are too big a man for this. Take in more fresh air . . . scatter your ecclesiastical harem. I do not say destroy your circle: I simply say enlarge it.

Spurgeon ignored the letter and advised his staff and pastor friends to do the same. Parker should have known that Spurgeon's power lay in concentration, not diffusion. He functioned best within his own household of faith, although he was generous to evangelicals in other denominations. "I am quite sure that the best way to promote union is to promote truth," he said in a sermon. "It will not do for us to be all united together by yielding to one another's mistakes." There are men like Parker, Campbell Morgan, and D. L. Moody, who seem to belong to all believers, regardless of denominational affiliation; but there are also men like Spurgeon, Maclaren, and Truett, who helped the evangelical cause best by concentrating on their own denominational ministry. We need both kinds of preachers, and one should not be quick to condemn the other.

You will want to read *Spurgeon: Heir of the Puritans* by Ernest W. Bacon, one of the best biographies; and also *A History of Spurgeon's Tabernacle* by Eric W. Hayden, who pastored the tabernacle for five years beginning in November 1956. The book is published in this country by Pilgrim Publications in Pasadena, Texas, and I urge you to secure it. It contains a wealth of information about the ministry of the tabernacle following Spurgeon's death, and the bibliographies of titles by and about Spurgeon are excellent.

But, above all else, read Spurgeon himself! Get a *complete* edition of his *Lectures to My Students* and read it carefully. Granted, some of the material is antiquated, but much is relevant to our ministry. "The Minister's Fainting Fits" and "The Need of Decision for the Truth" ought to be required reading for all ministerial students.

I enjoy reading *An All-Round Ministry*, a collection of Spurgeon's presidential addresses to the students and alumni of the Pastors' College. I say "enjoy reading," but I must confess that these messages have more than once driven me to my knees in confession and prayer. Perhaps they will do the same for you.

Spurgeon was a lover of good books, with a library of some twelve thousand volumes. His views on books are found in the delightful volume *Commenting and Commentaries*, first published in 1876 and reprinted by Banner of Truth in 1969 (the new edition includes a complete index of Spurgeon's sermons). If nothing else, simply enjoy reading his comments, many of which he must have written with a broad smile on his face. Naturally he favors the Puritans; but he had some kind words for writers of other schools—except the dispensationalists.

Of C. H. M.'s *Genesis* he wrote, "Precious and edifying reflections marred by peculiarities." Of *Exodus*, "Not free from Plymouth errors, yet remarkably suggestive." He warned that *Leviticus* "should be read cautiously." By the time he got to *Numbers*, he used both barrels: "Like the other notes of C. H. M., they need filtering. Good as they are, their *Darbyism* gives them an unpleasant and unhealthy savour." His comments about Darby's books are not flattering: "Too mystical for ordinary minds," he wrote about *Practical Reflections on the Psalms*. "If the author would write in plain English his readers would probably discover that there is nothing very valuable in his remarks." Of that other great Brethren writer, William Kelly, Spurgeon wrote: "Mr. Kelly's authoritative style has no weight with us. We do not call these lectures expounding, but confounding." Four decades later, C. I. Scofield would preach often in Spurgeon's pulpit during the pastorate of A. C. Dixon, who, by the way, had resigned from Moody Church to go to London.

One could go on and on about Spurgeon, citing facts and recalling anecdotes; but this is something you need to experience yourself. Plunge right into his sermons, his autobiography, and his other writings, and revel in the grace of God that was so real to this mighty preacher. Like all of us, Spurgeon had his faults and weaknesses, but he magnified God's grace and glorified God's son. We cannot all be Spurgeons, but we can all be faithful, as he was, in preaching the gospel of Jesus Christ.

7

Dwight L. Moody
1837–1899

Dwight Lyman Moody was perhaps the most remarkable Christian layman America ever produced.

Yes, I said "layman," because D. L. Moody was never ordained, nor did he ever have any formal training for the ministry. He preferred to be called "Mr. Moody," and he readily admitted his educational limitations. In fact, whenever a group of preachers met with him, Moody usually asked them pointed questions about the Bible and the interpretation of difficult passages. "I have never been through a college or a theological seminary," he once said to a gathering of London pastors, "and I have invited you here to get all the valuable teaching I can out of you to use in my work!"

And he readily admitted when his interpretations were wrong and his sermons had to be changed!

One time Moody invited Dr. Henry Weston of Crozier Seminary to be one of the speakers at his Northfield Conference. (Dr. Weston was one of the original editors of the *Scofield Reference Bible*.) As Weston stepped to the pulpit, Moody picked up one of the platform chairs, stepped off the platform, and sat right in front of the pulpit, literally at the preacher's feet.

Dr. Weston began to expound the Word, and suddenly Moody exclaimed, "There goes one of my sermons!" Weston stopped and asked the evangelist what he had meant by that statement. Moody explained that Weston's exposition had shown him that his own sermon on that text had been built on a misinterpretation and was now useless.

Weston continued to preach, and Moody said it again, "There goes another!" Weston smiled and kept right on speaking, because in his seminary classes the students had used Moody's sermons to challenge their professor's interpretations—and now the situation was reversed!

As I review the life of D. L. Moody, I am again amazed to discover how many important servants of God were influenced by this energetic Yankee's life and ministry. Ira Sankey, Moody's soloist, would probably have died an unknown Internal Revenue collector had Moody not recruited him. The saintly F. B. Meyer, proper British pastor, had his life transformed through meeting and working with Moody. The godly American pastor, S. D. Gordon—whose series of *Quiet Talk* books is still popular—was converted in Moody's campaign in Philadelphia (1875–76). Moody laid hands on intellectual Reuben Archer Torrey and God made a soul-winning evangelist out of him. Spurgeon's gifted assistant, W. Y. Fullerton, gladly admitted that he "discovered his life's business"—the winning of the lost—at Moody's Belfast meetings in 1874. And the great expositor Dr. G. Campbell Morgan was "discovered" by Moody and brought to America before Morgan's gifts were really appreciated in Britain. (In all fairness, we must admit that Moody himself was "discovered" in Britain before he became popular in America.)

Dr. A. T. Pierson estimated conservatively that Moody brought the gospel to 100 million people during his lifetime—without radio, television, or even a public address system! And it is remarkable to discover some of the people who sat in his congregations—a lad named Harry Ironside, for one. When Moody held his Los Angeles campaign in 1888, twelve-year-old Ironside was sitting in Hazzard's Pavilion, listening intently. Little did either of them realize that, for eighteen years (1930–48), Ironside would pastor Moody Church in Chicago.

When Moody was preaching in Denver, a young lad wanted to hear the evangelist but could not get into the building. "I'll get you in!" said a heavyset man at the back door. "Just hold on to my coattail." The man was D. L. Moody, and the boy was Paul Rader, who grew up to become one of America's greatest preachers and also a pastor of Moody Church (1915–21).

In the late 1800s, when Moody was preaching in western New York, a boy named Harry Emerson Fosdick was in the congregation—more than once! Apparently the gospel message did not impress the lad, for he grew up to become

America's leading liberal preacher and an opponent of the fundamentals of the faith.

How could this relatively unlearned shoe salesman become such a forceful and effective evangelist and teacher? Moody's success lay in his tremendous burden for the lost and a willingness to do whatever God asked of him. The life and ministry of this humble man of God is an example to us of what the Lord can do in the life of an ordinary person who is totally yielded to him.

Dwight L. Moody was born in Northfield, Massachusetts, on February 5, 1837. When he was four months old, young Victoria was crowned Queen of England, and Moody lived through almost all of the Victorian era. He died December 22, 1899, and Victoria died January 22, 1901.

The Moody family was poor, and the situation became even worse when their father died in 1841, leaving their mother with seven children. Twins were born to her just a month after her husband died. The creditors swooped down on her, taking even the fuel from the woodpile. One especially cruel neighbor tried to foreclose on the mortgage. (Forty years later, Moody bought the man out!)

When Moody was seventeen years old, he went to Boston to work in his uncle's shoe store. Sam Holton made his nephew promise that he would attend Sunday school and church, which young Dwight dutifully did. Fortunately, he had a teacher who was burdened for the lost. On April 25, 1855, Edward Kimball visited Moody at the store and led him to faith in Jesus Christ. (Seventeen years later, Moody would lead Kimball's son to the Savior.)

"I was in a new world," said Moody as he recalled the experience. "The next morning the sun shone brighter and the birds sang sweeter . . . it was the most delicious joy that I'd ever known."[1]

A month later, Moody applied for membership in the Mt. Vernon Church, but he was rejected because he simply could not answer the questions put to him by the committee. One officer told him, "Young man, you can serve the Lord better by keeping still!" It took Moody a year to join the church; he was finally admitted on May 4, 1856.

Four months later he was in Chicago, selling shoes for the Wiswall Company on Lake Street. Moody was nineteen years old, a hard worker and a growing Christian; and, like Joseph in Egypt, he prospered because the Lord was with him.

Moody joined the Plymouth Congregational Church where Dr. J. E. Roy was pastor. He rented five pews and filled them with young men Sunday after Sunday. One day he walked into a little mission on North Wells Street and told the superintendent that he wanted to teach a Sunday school class. Apologetically, the superintendent confessed that he had almost as many teachers as students, so Moody decided to recruit his own class. The next Sunday he showed up with eighteen ragged pupils, thus doubling the size of the school.

"That was the happiest Sunday I have ever known," Moody later stated. "I had found out what my mission was."

During the summer of 1858, he taught his growing class on the shores of Lake Michigan. When winter set in, he moved them into an old, abandoned saloon on Market Street. By 1859 there were one thousand pupils in Moody's Sunday school, and the creative ministry of their leader had won for him the title "Crazy Moody." In fact, when Moody returned to Northfield for a visit in January 1860, his uncle Zeb Allen said he was crazy! To compensate for this kind of opposition, however, something very special happened on November 25, 1860—Abraham Lincoln visited Moody's school and commended his work.

In June of that year Moody learned a lesson that helped transform his life and direct him into his future ministry. One of his faithful teachers was dying of tuberculosis and was greatly burdened for his pupils. Before he went to heaven, he wanted to be sure all of them were converted. The man was too weak to visit them alone, so Moody went along. For ten days, the two men visited home after home; and at the end of that time, they saw each of the children won to the Lord. When the teacher left for his widowed mother's home to die, the entire class was at the railroad station, singing songs about heaven.

This experience made a lasting impression on Moody. From it he got "the strongest impulse for trying to bring souls to Christ." Being successful in business meant less and less to him. The only business that counted was God's business—winning the lost to Jesus Christ.

During the Civil War, Moody ministered effectively to the soldiers. In fact, this was his training ground for later ministry. He gradually overcame his shyness in public speaking and learned how to deal personally with people in great need. Moody built a chapel at Camp Douglas (where the Illinois Institute of Technology now stands) and saw that the gospel was preached to the men. He made nine visits to the front. He was on hand at Pittsburg Landing, Shiloh, and Murfreesboro, and was one of the first to enter Richmond.

Moody prospered as a shoe salesman and had saved $7,000—quite a sum in that day! He decided it was time he thought about marriage. He had noticed a lovely Christian girl teaching in the Sunday school. Her name was Emma Revell, and her father had been a British shipbuilder who had come to America to make a new beginning. Dwight and Emma were engaged in 1860, and on August 28, 1862, they were married. If the name *Revell* sounds familiar to you, it is because Emma's brother, Fleming H. Revell, founded the Christian publishing firm that bore his name. In fact, he went into publishing primarily to make Moody's songbooks and sermons available at a popular price to a wider audience. D. L. Moody was probably the originator of the Christian paperback.

As Moody's Sunday school prospered, he faced a problem. Most of his converts did not feel at home in the established churches of the city. They wanted to be with Mr. Moody. Always the innovator and the pioneer, Moody built the Illinois Street Independent Church and laid hands on a fellow named Wheeler to be the pastor. Of course, nobody doubted who the leader of the church was.

Moody was now in the Lord's business full-time. He allowed himself to be appointed to the Illinois State Sunday School Union Board. Always the activist, Moody never did shine while serving on committees; however, his presence certainly kept everybody else on their toes. In 1866 he was elected president of the YMCA in Chicago, a position he held until 1870. In that day, the "Y" was an evangelical ministry, seeking to reach the young people in the city. It was a perfect base of ministry for a man like Moody.

Despite his early successes, D. L. Moody still had some important lessons to learn about the Bible and about evangelism. At that moment God was preparing the man who would teach Moody these lessons. And the truths that would revolutionize Moody's ministry were to come—not from the great theologians and preachers of the day—but from an ex-prizefighter in Great Britain.

"I do not expect to visit this country again." Dwight L. Moody made that statement shortly after arriving in England in March 1867. He had been seasick during the voyage from America and was also a bit discouraged with the "dull and formal" church life in England. In short, he was homesick.

But Mr. Moody was wrong in his evaluation. During his ministry he would visit Britain seven times, and his fourth visit would last more than two years and result in thousands coming to Christ. In fact, it was Britain that really discovered Moody and Sankey and made their names household words before the men were famous in America.

During that first visit, Moody had practically no public ministry. He went to the Metropolitan Tabernacle and heard Charles Spurgeon preach. Although an usher tried to keep Moody out of the Tabernacle because he didn't have a ticket, the quick-talking shoe salesman argued his way in. Spurgeon was one of his spiritual heroes, and Moody was not about to visit London without hearing him. Moody was greatly moved by the message from "an untrained man" like himself.

In the weeks that followed, Moody also met John Nelson Darby (founder of the Plymouth Brethren movement) and George Müller (pioneer of the famous "faith ministry" with orphans).

Moody gave a brief address at the anniversary breakfast of the Aldersgate YMCA in London. He was introduced as "our American cousin, the Reverend Mr. Moody from Chicago."

"The vice-chairman has made two mistakes," Moody said in reply. "To begin with, I'm not 'the Reverend Mr. Moody' at all. I'm plain Dwight L. Moody, a Sabbath school worker. And then I'm not your 'American cousin.' By the grace of God, I'm your brother, who is interested with you in our Father's work for his children."

In the speech that followed, Moody "unstarched" the British brethren, won many friends, offended a few saints, and started a fresh wind blowing. The noon prayer meetings at the YMCA took on new power and blessing, thanks to the influence of Moody. This brief contact with some of Britain's religious leaders would bring rich dividends in Moody's later ministry, particularly the 1873–75 campaign.

But in retrospect, the most important man he met on that trip was the ex-prizefighter Harry Moorehouse. Converted out of a life of great sin, Moorehouse had become a bold evangelist for the Lord. He and Moody had a great deal in common, but Moody was to learn from Moorehouse two important lessons.

"If you are ever in Chicago, plan to preach at my church," Moody casually told Moorehouse, and then Moody forgot the matter completely. But Moorehouse did not forget. No sooner had Moody returned to Chicago than he received a letter from Moorehouse, informing his new friend that he had arrived in New York and would be coming to Chicago to preach! Moody had to be out of the city, so he told the church officers to let the young man preach.

When Moody returned home, he asked Emma how the British preacher had done, and she gave her husband an enthusiastic report. "He proves everything he says from the Bible," she said, "and he has preached both nights from the same text—John 3:16." Always ready to learn new truths and pick up new ideas, Moody went to the meeting and was amazed to see his own people carrying Bibles and using them during the message. Moorehouse began at John 3:16 and took the people from Genesis to Revelation as he talked about the love of God and the divine plan of redemption.

Privately, Moorehouse gently rebuked Moody. "Learn to preach God's words instead of your own. He will make you a great power for good." Then Moorehouse showed Moody how to use the Bible and trace the great themes of Scripture. It was like a second conversion for Moody. He purchased a *Cruden's Concordance* and began to get up two or three hours before breakfast so that he might read and study the Bible. Years later, at the 1887 Northfield Conference, Moody said: "Take up the Bible, with a concordance. I believe Alexander Cruden did more to open up the Bible than he could ever have dreamed."

But Moorehouse did more than teach Moody how to study the Bible. He taught him to love sinners to the Savior. Night after night, as the ex-prizefighter preached on John 3:16, he emphasized the love of God for lost men and women. As Moody listened, his eyes were opened and his heart was melted. "I never knew . . . that God loved us so much! This heart of mine began to thaw out; I could not hold back the tears."

From 1867 to the fall of 1871, Moody kept busy in Sunday school work and the program of the YMCA. He became a popular speaker at state Sunday school conventions and was even elected to various offices in the associations, including that of president of the Illinois State Sunday School Association.

In 1870 Moody made a second trip to Britain. That same year, at the "Y" convention in Indianapolis, he heard Ira Sankey sing and decided he was just the man he needed for his own ministry. "Where are you from?" Moody asked. "What is your business? Are you married?" Sankey answered Moody's questions, wondering what he was driving at.

It took Moody six months to convince Sankey that evangelism was his calling; but the man finally yielded, and the team of "Moody and Sankey" was born.

One story about Sankey must be repeated. While serving in the Union army, Sankey was on guard duty one night and felt inspired to sing a hymn. What he did not know was that he was in the sights of a Confederate rifleman who, when he heard the song, lowered his rifle and did not shoot. If ever a man had been "compassed about with songs of deliverance" (see Ps. 32:7), it was Ira Sankey.

It appeared that everything was now in place, and Moody could move ahead in Sunday school work, the YMCA ministry, and the winning of souls. But something was still missing in Moody's life and ministry, and he had to experience some further crises before he would become the man God wanted him to be. If ever there was a busy man serving the Lord, it was Dwight L. Moody. But deep within, Moody knew that something was missing from his ministry.

Enter at this point two somewhat eccentric women, Aunt Sarah Cooke and Mrs. Hawxhurst, both of whom were identified with "the holiness movement" of greater Chicago and northern Indiana. Cooke belonged to the Free Methodist Church but fellowshipped widely with God's people and called herself simply "the handmaiden of the Lord."

"Mr. Moody was an earnest, whole-souled worker," Sarah Cooke wrote in her memoirs, *Wayside Sketches*, "but ever to me there seemed such a lack in his words. It seemed more the human, the natural energy and force of character of the man, than anything spiritual."[2]

Cooke and Hawxhurst often discussed Moody and his ministry and then decided to talk to the man himself. They told him that they were praying for him that he might receive the power of the Spirit. At first Moody was surprised at their concern and suggested that they pray for the lost. Then he became convicted and began to pray with the ladies every Friday afternoon.

"At every meeting," Sarah Cooke reported, "he would get more earnest, in agony of desire for this fullness of the Spirit."

But before the "fire" of God's power came upon him, Moody experienced another kind of fire, for on October 8,

1871, the great Chicago fire broke out. From Belden Avenue on the north to 12th Street on the south, and as far west as Halsted Street, the fire destroyed more than 17,000 buildings and property worth nearly $200 million.

Moody was preaching that night at Farwell Hall on the theme "What Will You Do with Jesus?" He admitted later that what he did that night was foolish—he ended the message by asking the people to take a week to decide and then come back to report their decision. But even while Sankey was singing the closing song (ironically it was "Today the Savior Calls"), the noise of fire engines and warning bells drowned out the meeting. Moody dismissed the crowd and set about doing what he could to rescue his family and a few possessions.

The Moody family found refuge with Horatio Spafford, the author of the hymn "It Is Well with My Soul." Later Moody said that the fire had taken from him "everything but my reputation and my Bible." When a well-meaning friend said, "Moody, I hear you lost everything!" Moody opened his Bible to Revelation 21:7 and said, "Well, you understood wrong. I have a good deal more than I lost!" Then he read the verse: "He that overcometh shall inherit all things; and I will be his God."

With his family cared for, Moody left for the East Coast to preach, rest, and raise money to replace his church building. It was while ministering in Theodore Cuyler's church in Brooklyn that Moody had his life-changing experience and the power of the Spirit came upon him. He was walking down Wall Street in New York City, mulling over the impotence of his preaching and the failure of his fund-raising program, when the Spirit of God filled him.

"Oh, what a day!" he later reported. "I cannot describe it; I seldom refer to it; it is almost too sacred an experience to name. . . . I can only say that God revealed Himself to me, and I had such an experience of His love that I had to ask Him to stay His hand."

It is unfortunate that some groups have tried to use Moody's experience to promote their own special views of the baptism of the Spirit and speaking in tongues. There is no evidence that D. L. Moody ever spoke in tongues, and during his many campaigns in Great Britain, he and Sankey always avoided the people who promoted tongues and prophesying. If somebody in a meeting began to speak out or swoon, Moody would either call for a hymn or close the meeting.

One of the leading specialists on the theology of D. L. Moody is my friend Dr. Stanley Gundry, whose definitive book *Love Them In: The Proclamation Theology of D. L. Moody* should be in every pastor's library. Originally published by Moody Press, the book was reprinted by Baker Books.

Dr. Gundry says:

One must proceed cautiously when examining Moody's statements on this matter (the filling of the Spirit), for it is all too easy to impose upon Moody's statements a meaning that he did not intend. . . . Moody himself seldom went into the details of his 1871 experience, or at least existing sermons seldom give the details. But on those rare occasions when he did, he described it as a filling, a baptism or an anointing that came upon him when he was in a cold state. His selfish ambitions in preaching had been surrendered, and he then received power by which to do his work for Christ.[3]

Moody returned to the rather dismal "revival" meeting at Cuyler's church, and the fire began to burn. More than one hundred people professed faith in Christ, and the blessings spread to other congregations. Moody was preaching the same messages, but his preaching contained a new tenderness, and the power of God was evident in the meetings.

Something also happened to Moody, the fund-raiser. Instead of depending on his own experience as a salesman, Moody began to trust God for guidance as he approached people with his needs. He was still aggressive, but in a new way. Before long he had the needed funds to replace the church building. On December 24, 1871, he dedicated the new tabernacle with more than 1,000 children and their parents assisting him.

Perhaps this is a good place to mention the history of the church that Mr. Moody founded in 1864. It was originally called the Illinois Street Independent Church, with Mr. Wheeler as the pastor. Of course, everybody knew that Mr. Moody was their leader, but he was not an ordained minister. From 1866 to 1869 J. H. Harwood pastored the church, but there was no regular pastor from 1869 to 1871. Moody had many friends who enjoyed assisting in the work, so there was always somebody in the pulpit. Often Moody did the preaching himself.

After the fire, the new structure was called the North Side Tabernacle, and in 1876 the church relocated to Chicago Avenue and LaSalle Street and became the Chicago Avenue Church. The esteemed pastors were William J. Erdman (1876–78), Charles M. Morton (1878, 1879), George C. Needham (1879–81), Charles F. Goss (1885–90), and Charles A. Blanchard (1891–93). From 1894 to 1906, Reuben Archer Torrey pastored the church, which was renamed Moody Church in 1901. Mr. Moody would never have put his name on the church, but it seemed to be an appropriate way to honor his memory after his death.

Beginning in 1889, the newly founded Chicago Evangelistic Society (later Moody Bible Institute) used the church's facilities, and Dr. R. A. Torrey served as both pastor and superintendent of the school. When Torrey left in 1906 to start the Church of the Open Door in Los Angeles, Dr. A. C. Dixon became pastor (1906–11). One of America's greatest preachers, Paul Rader, became pastor in 1915, and the church moved a mile north on LaSalle Street to North Avenue, where a 5,000-seat tabernacle was built. Rader preached to thousands of people night after night, and multitudes were saved.

Rader resigned in 1921, and P. W. Philpott accepted the pulpit, remaining until 1929. During his ministry the congregation tore down the old tabernacle and, in 1925, dedicated the present building that is officially named the Moody Memorial Church. For eighteen fruitful years (1930–48), Dr. H. A. Ironside ministered the Word to large congregations, and on every Sunday except two he saw public decisions for Christ.

S. Franklin Logsden followed Dr. Ironside as pastor. Logsden was succeeded by Dr. Alan Redpath from England. From 1966 to 1971, Dr. George Sweeting was pastor. I had the privilege of succeeding Dr. Sweeting, serving from 1971 to 1978. The present pastor is Dr. Erwin Lutzer, a former instructor at Moody Bible Institute.

Whenever former Moody pastors or Moody church "alumni" get together, there are often spirited discussions about what Mr. Moody would have done had he lived longer. Would he have approved the construction of a 4,000-seat cathedral-type church building? Would he perhaps have scattered the congregation to various locations in Chicago, to build fifty or one hundred soul-winning churches? Paul Rader wanted to build a "skyscraper" with an auditorium for 2,500 people and classrooms and offices for the church; and then he planned to rent the rest of the structure out to help pay the bills!

Unless Mr. Moody tells us in heaven, we will never know what he would have done; therefore, it is useless to speculate. We do know that both Moody Church and Moody Bible Institute, with its many ministries, have been used by God over the years to bless countless people around the world.

Moody made another trip to Britain in 1872, during which he was introduced to "dispensational truth" and met evangelist Henry Varley. It was Varley who said to Moody (and this seems to be the accurate version): "Moody, the world has yet to see what God can do with and for and through and in a man who is fully and wholly consecrated to Him."

Varley did not remember making the statement, but Moody never forgot it.

One of the ministers asked Moody to preach at a church in Arundel Square, London, and that service turned into a two-week meeting during which four hundred people professed faith in Christ. Part of the secret behind the harvest was the praying of Marianne Adlard, a bedridden girl who had read about Moody in a newspaper and had been praying daily that he would come to her church and preach. God answered her prayers, and Moody caught a new vision of what God could do through him in Britain.

In fact, it was a crisis experience for him. As a result, he determined to concentrate on evangelism and give himself completely to the winning of lost souls. The result was the great campaign of 1873–75.

"I go where I can do the most good. That is what I am after. It is souls I want—it is souls I want!"

Moody spoke those words to some British friends in 1873. He had recently arrived in Britain, responding to an invitation from three leading English Christians—Henry Bewley, Cuthbert Bainbridge and William Pennefather. To his dismay, he discovered that Bainbridge and Pennefather were both dead and that Bewley was not expecting him.

But Moody was not the kind of man who quit easily. He had in his pocket a letter from George Bennet, who was secretary of the YMCA at York, so he wired Bennet that he was coming. The man was shocked by the news and informed Moody that it would take weeks for them to get ready for a meeting. Bennet's arguments meant nothing to Moody, who promptly went to York and started preaching the Word, with Sankey singing his way into the hearts of the people.

The British congregations were suspicious and for a time kept their distance. "One has an organ and performs on that," went the report. "The other tells stories." And everybody waited to see what the "catch" was and how these uninvited American guests would make a profit out of the meetings. Attendance was not large, and the spirit of the meetings was nothing exciting.

Then God touched a pastor's heart, and the whole atmosphere began to change. The young pastor of the Priory Street Baptist Chapel was brought under deep conviction at the noon prayer meeting. He had been "beating the air" in his ministry, and when Moody had preached on the Holy Spirit, the pastor realized his need and how God could meet it. That man was F. B. Meyer, whose ministry of the Word would be greatly used around the world and whose many books minister to hearts even today.

Meyer even permitted Moody to use his church building for extra services, and by now the tide was beginning to flow in. A large crowd came to hear Moody at the Corn Exchange, and one of the leading religious newspapers in England began to report the meetings. F. B. Meyer was so blessed with his new vision of evangelism and ministry that his enthusiasm offended some of his officers, and he was asked to leave the church. "This is not a gospel shop!" the irate officers told him. God opened the way for him to establish a new church in Leicester, "Melbourne Hall," which still maintains a faithful witness.

After the ministry at York, Moody and Sankey moved to Sunderland and then Newcastle. Their friend Harry Moorehouse joined them and shared in the meetings. It was at Newcastle that *Sacred Songs and Solos* was first issued, published on September 16 by Marshall, Morgan, and Scott. Known as the "Sankey Hymnbook," this volume was just what Moody needed in his meetings, as most of the church hymnals did not contain gospel songs with an evangelistic emphasis.

Since that time, more than ten million copies of *Sacred Songs and Solos* have been sold. When the initial royalties started to come in, Moody offered them to his British friends for whatever ministries they chose; but they refused the money. So Moody sent the money back to Chicago where it was used to complete the Chicago Avenue Church building.

The tide continued to come in, so the team decided to invade traditional, evangelical Scotland; on November 23, they opened a campaign in Edinburgh. It was not an encouraging beginning. For one thing, Moody was ill with tonsillitis; for another, Sankey's organ was in need of repairs. But they started the meetings, and God began to bless.

Let me interrupt this report with an interesting sidelight. On October 19, just a few weeks before Moody and Sankey arrived, the leading "spiritual giant" of Scotland, Dr. R. S. Candlish, died. Before he died, he predicted that there would come to Scotland "a great blessing which should not be despised, though it come strangely." Moody and Sankey were the "strange" bearers of that blessing.

Here's a humorous sidelight on the Edinburgh meetings. Sankey finally got his organ repaired (the Scots called it "a chest of whistles") and sang the gospel in the meetings. At one point, it was necessary to hold two meetings across the street from each other in order to accommodate the crowds. Sankey would sing in one church while Moody preached in the other, and then they would exchange places.

As Sankey began to sing and play his organ in the one meeting, a faithful Presbyterian lady jumped up and ran from the meeting, shouting, "Let me oot! Let me oot! What would John Knox think of the like of ye?" She was offended, of course, by Sankey's use of a musical instrument in a church. She then went across the street to the other meeting, and when Sankey appeared to sing there, she jumped up and ran out again, still shouting, "Let me oot! Let me oot! What would John Knox think of the like of ye?"

It is worth noting that Sankey sang "The Ninety and Nine" for the first time in the Edinburgh campaign. The words were written by a frail Scottish lady, Elizabeth C. Clephane, who lived near Edinburgh. Sankey had found the poem in a newspaper he had purchased at the train depot and, impressed with the message, had put the clipping in his pocket. After preaching on the Good Shepherd, Moody turned to Sankey and asked him to sing an appropriate song. Asking God for help, Sankey put the words on his organ, struck A-flat, and composed the tune as he went along. Moody then gave his invitation, and many "lost sheep" entered the inquiry room to find the Shepherd.

On February 8 the campaign moved to Glasgow, but all was not well. One of Scotland's most famous preachers, the Reverend John Kennedy ("The Spurgeon of the Highlands"), opposed Mr. Moody's ministry. The fact that some 3,000 persons had been received into the Edinburgh churches as a result of Moody's work did not impress Kennedy. He published a pamphlet "proving" that it was not scriptural for Moody to use "human hymns" instead of the Psalms, to play the organ in a church, or to invite sinners into inquiry rooms.

Not all of the leading clergy were opposed to the campaign, however, among them the saintly Andrew Bonar, noted pastor and special friend of Robert Murray McCheyne. "The tide of real revival in Edinburgh has been stirring up all of us," he wrote in his journal on January 1, 1874. On February 10, he wrote: "This city has been at last visited; Moody and Sankey, sent by the Lord." Bonar and many other pastors prayed earnestly that God would break through the religious complacency of the churches and that many sinners would come to the Savior.

God answered their prayers as the tide kept deepening. On February 24, some 101 men professed faith in Christ in one meeting! When the campaign closed on April 19, the record showed that there had been more than 6,000 professions of faith and that 7,000 persons had united with local churches. Bonar wrote in his journal that he had a communicant's class of fifty-two, all of them clear as to their salvation experience, and that fifty-four people came to the Lord's Table for the first time.

Moody and Sankey spent the summer months in the Scottish Highlands, ministering from town to town, and then in September moved to Ireland. In spite of some inclement weather and the prejudice of some Roman Catholic people, the meetings were a great success. Buildings were packed, and people responded to Moody's simple presentation of the gospel.

After five weeks in Belfast, the men moved their witness to Dublin where only one-fourth of the population was Protestant. The crowds came, however, even though the archbishop had issued an edict forbidding his people to attend. Even ridicule did not affect the ministry, as the following story proves.

A couple of clowns performing at a Dublin circus tried to ridicule the evangelists with this routine:

"I'm rather Moody tonight. How do you feel?"

"I feel rather Sankeymonious."

The audience began to hiss the so-called comedians and then began to sing "Hold the Fort."

For the most part, the Roman Catholic publications were sympathetic to the meetings. One editor wrote: "The deadly danger of the age comes upon us from the direction of Huxley and Darwin and Tyndall, rather than from Moody and Sankey." Moody's positive message carried the day, and the *British Weekly* called the meetings "a Pentecost."

The Irish campaign closed on November 29, and Moody then preached in Manchester during December, in Birmingham in January, and in Liverpool in February. The crowds came and people were converted, although not as many as Moody had hoped. On March 9 he tackled London with its three million people. Once again his biggest problem was with the clergy, so Moody held an informal session to answer their questions.

"How are you paid?" one minister asked.

"I have money enough for myself right in my pocket," said Moody, "and do not ask for a cent." (The fact was that Moody had single-handedly raised thousands of dollars for the construction of YMCA buildings and missions in Britain.)

"I am a ritualist," said another minister. "Will you send me all my proper and rightful converts?"

Moody replied, "I am not here to divide up the profits but to get as many as I can to give their hearts to Jesus Christ."

It seems that every Christian evangelist, from Peter to Martin Luther to John Wesley to Moody to those of our present day, has had his greatest problems with the ministers who should have been out winning the lost themselves.

An entire book could be written about the miracles of the London campaign. Wealthy sportsman Edward Studd came to Christ through Moody's ministry, and eight years later his son C. T. Studd trusted Christ when Moody preached at Cambridge. Fifteen thousand men attended a special "men only" meeting and many of them found Christ. It was estimated that 2.5 million people heard Moody and Sankey during the campaign and that the men conducted 285 different public meetings. The total budget ran $140,000!

On August 4, 1875, Moody left for home, arriving in the United States ten days later. It had been a triumphant campaign for Christ. He had won the battle for Britain.

Before we leave Moody and Sankey, let's try to answer the question that many people asked then and still ask today: what was the secret of their success, not only in their British campaign but also in their ministry in general? When you read the reports and evaluations written in Moody's day, you start to get a composite answer that seems to be valid.

To begin with, Moody himself was a Spirit-filled man who was burdened for souls. He had no interest in making money. He was not intimidated by "important people," nor was he afraid to try something new. In fact, Moody stands as one of the great innovators in Christian ministry. If one approach did not work, being a good businessman, he tried another.

The meetings were undergirded with prayer. The noon prayer meeting was the most important meeting of the day to Moody. If it became dull or dead, he livened it up and got the people praying. "I'd rather be able to pray than to be a great preacher," he once said. "Jesus Christ never taught his disciples how to preach, but only how to pray."

Third, he worked in and through the church and encouraged ministers to forget their minor differences and work together to win the lost. This was not easy in Britain where the state church and the independents sometimes engaged in mutual suspicion and attack. "Satan separates," said Moody. "God unites. Love binds us together."

Moody used the Bible and kept the Bible before the people. During the two years of the British campaign, publishers could hardly keep up with the demand for Bibles. "I have observed that Mr. Moody speaks to inquirers with an open Bible in his hands," wrote one reporter. Moody did not argue theology; he simply quoted the Bible and let God speak for himself.

Several leaders mentioned the order and atmosphere of the meetings as a factor in Moody's success. There was a spirit of worship, and ushers were trained to deal immediately with disturbances. When applause broke out in one meeting, it was instantly silenced; and often Moody would call for times of silent prayer and worship.

Everybody knew that Ira Sankey's music was a key factor in the blessing of God on the meetings. Even the dour Scots finally yielded to the wooing of the portable organ and songs of the American singer. One reporter wrote: "He spoils the Egyptians of their finest music and consecrates it to the service of the tabernacle." Both Moody and Sankey were courageous enough to use new hymns and gospel songs in spite of the opposition of the traditionalists.

The campaign seemed a failure at the start, but God worked in a remarkable way and gave Britain perhaps the greatest spiritual movement since the days of George Whitefield and John Wesley. And he did it through two ordinary men who would not quit but who trusted God to bless his Word.

God can still do that today in our land or in any land. Henry Varley's words are still true: "The world has yet to see what God can do with and for and through and in a man who is fully and wholly consecrated to Him."

8

Amy Carmichael
1867–1951

Let me describe some of the things she did, and then allow you to answer the question: "If she were a missionary from your church, would you support Amy Carmichael?"

She spent nearly sixty years in the field and never once came home to report to her board or to the people who supported her.

While she went to the field under the authority of one board, she pretty much did her own thing and eventually started an organization of her own.

She went to the field to carry on one kind of ministry, but within a few years was carrying on an entirely different ministry that often got her into trouble with the law. At one time, she was in danger of serving seven years in prison for "assisting in the kidnapping of a child."

The reports that she sent out were often not believed by the people who read them. "Such things simply can't be!" they argued, but they were—and she proved it.

She did not ask for financial support, yet she saw every need met right on time. When people offered to sponsor part of her ministry, she suggested they support a different mission.

During the last twenty years of her ministry, she was practically an invalid, directing the work from her room.

My guess is that the average church would never have supported this kind of a missionary. She was too unpredictable and too independent. And perhaps the average mission board would have dropped her from their ranks after her first term. We like ministry work to be carried out in such a predictable way that there can be no surprises, no changes, no unexpected decisions that pioneer new territory for the gospel. It might upset the donors.

But Amy Carmichael was not put together that way. She simply did not fit into our modern world of interchangeable parts, because she was unique. She knew what God wanted her to do, and she did it. She was not a rebel; her board and co-laborers were full partners in the ministry. But she was one of the Lord's special servants, and he used her to accomplish a miracle ministry in southern India.

Amy Carmichael was born on December 16, 1867, in County Down, Northern Ireland. Her father, along with her uncle, owned and managed several flour mills, so the family was fairly comfortable. They came from Covenanter stock and took the things of the Lord seriously. Amy had a happy childhood, and, while a student at a Wesleyan Methodist school in 1883, she trusted Christ.

Changes in the milling business forced the family to move to Belfast. Amy's father died in 1885, and this greatly altered both the finances and the future of the family. Mrs. Carmichael was a woman of strong faith; in fact, much of her "apostolic spirit" rubbed off on her daughter. One particular incident illustrates this.

It was Sunday morning, and Mrs. Carmichael and the children were returning home from church. They met "a poor pathetic old woman" who was burdened with a heavy bundle. Instantly, Amy and her two brothers relieved the woman of her bundle, took her arms, and helped her along. At first the icy stares of the "proper Presbyterians" embarrassed them, but then the Lord moved in and the whole scene changed.

Into Amy's mind flashed Paul's words from 1 Corinthians 3 about "gold, silver, precious stones, wood, hay, stubble; . . . the fire shall try every man's work of what sort it is" (vv. 12, 13). In later years Amy wrote, "We went on. I said nothing to anyone, but I knew that something had happened that had changed life's values. Nothing could ever matter again but the things that were eternal."

In September 1886, some friends invited Amy to Glasgow, where she attended meetings along the lines of the Keswick Convention. For many months, she had been struggling with the problem of how to live a holy life, and she found the answer at the Glasgow meetings. It was not the message of the two speakers that got through to her but the closing prayer of the chairman. He paraphrased Jude 1:24: "O Lord, we know that Thou art able to keep us from falling!" Those words brought light into the darkness, and Amy Carmichael entered into a life of faith and victory.

But holy living was not a luxury to her: it meant sacrifice and ministry. She had no time for Christians who went from meeting to meeting and soaked up Bible truth but never reached out to share Christ with others. Amy was burdened for the girls who worked in the mills, and she had already started a ministry for them at one of the local churches. But the work was growing and in some ways interfering with the church's program (Amy always was one to raise dust).

She decided that, if God wanted her to start a special work, he alone could provide the funds and the laborers; so she began to pray. Little did she realize that this experience with The Welcome (the hall that she built) would prepare her for years of ministry by faith alone. God did provide the funds, and a building was put up just for ministry to the girls at the mills. Many came to know Christ, and many were protected from lives of sin because of the influence of the ministry. This would be Amy Carmichael's emphasis for the rest of her life—to reach out to the downcast and rejected, to love them, win them to Christ, and build them up to help others.

In later years, Amy said that there were three crises in her early life: her conversion, her entrance into the life of faith, and her call to be a missionary. That third crisis took place on January 13, 1892, not in some dramatic way, but simply as she waited quietly before the Lord. He made it clear to her that she was to give her life to him as a missionary and permit him to direct her just as he pleased.

There were obstacles, not the least of which was her commitment to help care for elderly Robert Wilson, an old friend of the family and the chairman of the British Keswick movement. She shared these concerns with her mother and Mr. Wilson, and step by step, the Lord began to open the way. On March 3, 1893, she sailed for Japan, the first missionary sent out by the Keswick Convention.

She had some remarkable experiences in Japan, ministering through an interpreter; but Japan was not to be her permanent field. A serious illness forced her to go to China for rest, and then to Ceylon (now Sri Lanka). Can you imagine a church foreign missions committee discussing her situation and wondering if she could be trusted? By the end of 1894, she was back in England; but a year later, on November 9, 1895, she landed in India, and there she remained until her death on January 18, 1951.

Amy was under the authority of the Church of England Zenana Missionary Society, so she entered into their ministry with zeal. But she noted that many of the missionaries reported no converts—in fact, *expected* none. She also noticed that the missionary community was separated in every way from the people they were trying to reach.

While in Japan, Amy had adopted native dress (as Hudson Taylor did in China) and had sought to identify with the people. But she had not come to India to create problems; so she went on with her work, always seeking the mind of Christ in her decisions.

Then something happened that dramatically changed Amy Carmichael's life and ministry. On March 6, 1901, little

Preena, a seven-year-old girl, fled from one of the temples into the mission compound and begged to be protected. It was then that Amy uncovered one of the ugliest hidden sores on "Mother India's" body, the secret traffic in temple girls. She learned how fathers and mothers sold their daughters to different gods, turning the precious girls into temple prostitutes.

Infuriated by what Satan was doing to these dear girls, Amy declared war. How many battles she fought on her knees, wrestling for the bodies and souls of these helpless children! How many times she and her associates risked their lives, and faced arrest and imprisonment, in order to snatch some pleading child from the jaws of defilement and destruction. One by one, other girls found their way to *Amma* (the Tamil word for "mother"), and she courageously protected them. By 1904 there were seventeen children under her care, and then the Lord opened the way for her to receive and minister to babies. In 1918 they opened the boy's work, for the money-hungry idolaters sold boys to the temple gods just as they sold girls.

If you want to enter into the excitement of pioneer missions, then read Amy Carmichael's *Gold Cord*, the story of the Dohnavur Fellowship. Frank Houghton's excellent biography, *Amy Carmichael of Dohnavur*, contains many of the exciting stories that grew out of the new ministry of saving temple children. Both books have been reprinted by Christian Literature Crusade; in fact, many of Amy Carmichael's books are available from that publisher.

Amma greatly admired the work of the China Inland Mission, and, in many ways, patterned herself after Hudson

Taylor. She did not solicit funds. When people asked to have the privilege of sponsoring a child, she refused their help. All funds went into the mission account to be dispensed as the Lord directed. The many workers God brought to her side were not paid salaries, and the mission never borrowed money or went into debt. While Amy did not criticize ministries that had other policies, she preferred to work as the Lord had led her.

She was especially careful about selecting workers. That was one reason for the no-salary policy. Many Indians would have gladly been baptized and worked for the mission in order to make a living. "Guard your gate" was one of her favorite warnings, and she heeded it herself. Some of her friends and supporters often were surprised when she rejected applicants who, to them, seemed ideally suited for the ministry; but later events always proved her right. She prayed men and women into places of service, trusting the Lord to prepare them, provide for them, and protect them.

Protection was especially important, not only because of the Indian climate and unsanitary conditions, but even more because of the idolatry and demonism. Satan and his armies attacked the people and the ministry at Dohnavur in ways that make these experiences read like events from the book of Acts. The secret of victory? The Word of God and prayer!

Amma and her associates practiced John 15:7, trusting God to guide them by the Word and provide for their needs one day at a time. I think it would be good for some of us to get acquainted with Amy Carmichael's principles for prayer:

1. We don't need to explain to our Father things that are known to him.
2. We don't need to press him, as if we had to deal with an unwilling God.
3. We don't need to suggest to him what to do, for he himself knows what to do.

If all of us took these principles to heart, think of the religious speeches that would be silenced in many prayer meetings.

Amy Carmichael cautioned her helpers to "leave a margin" in their lives. We have all been reminded to "beware of the barrenness of a busy life." As I read Amy Carmichael's books, I am amazed at the broad scope of her reading, not only in many translations of the Bible, but in the mystics, the church fathers, even the Greek philosophers. To her, reading was an enriching experience, a time for relaxation and renewal and not just escape.

On October 24, 1931, Amy Carmichael suffered a serious fall. Other complications set in, and she had to end her usual activity. She was physically limited to her room and an occasional veranda stroll, but that did not limit her ministry. In the next twenty years she wrote thirteen books and many letters, and she directed the work of the mission through her capable associates.

In 1948 she experienced a second fall, and from then until her Homegoing she was confined to her bed. But she was constantly at the throne of grace, and God answered her prayers. God is still answering those prayers, for the

Dohnavur Fellowship continues to minister effectively in southern India.

Amy Carmichael wrote thirty-five books of various kinds—the story of the Fellowship, poems, stories about the children who were rescued, devotionals, and messages for those who suffer. Many of them have been republished by Christian Literature Crusade and should be available in your local Christian bookstore. Not everyone takes to Miss Carmichael's writing; in fact, I must confess that it took me many years to learn to appreciate her style and message (*I* was the one who had to grow.).

His Thoughts Said . . . His Father Said is excellent for times of meditative pondering. *Thou Givest . . . They Gather* is another fine devotional book, compiled from her writings after her death. Two encouraging books for suffering people are *Candles in the Dark* and *Rose from Brier*. When *God's Missionary* was published, it upset many people because of its emphasis on devotion and personal discipline. It still upsets readers—but perhaps they need to be upset. Books about Indian women reached through the Dohnavur ministry include *Mimosa, Ponnammal, Kohila,* and *Ploughed Under. Edges of His Ways* is a daily devotional book that is intellectually stimulating and spiritually rewarding.

"We were committed to things that we must not expect everyone to understand" was the way *Amma* explained her ministry and was also the reason why some devout evangelicals kept at a distance. "The work will never go deeper than we have gone ourselves" was her explanation of why some workers did not remain and why others refused to come. She did not try to please everybody or solicit anybody's support. The work was God's work, and he alone could prosper it. No high-powered machinery, no Madison Avenue promotion, no attempts to compete with other ministries either for funds or personnel.

Amy Carmichael depended on God for day-by-day and hour-by-hour direction. God spoke to her through the Word, through the pages of her dog-eared *Daily Light*, through the impulses of the heart; yes, on occasion, even through dreams. Seminary professors who write learned books about how to interpret the Bible would probably call her use of Bible texts or parts of texts superstitious, but they would have to confess that she was a woman led by God and blessed by God. She exercised a simple-hearted faith in God, nurtured by a wholehearted love for God, and her Father saw to it that she was cared for.

Here is a "Confession of Love" that she drew up for a group of Indian girls who banded together to serve Christ. Perhaps it best says to us just what Amy Carmichael believed about Christian life and service.

> My Vow: Whatsoever Thou sayest unto me, by Thy grace I will do it.
>
> My Constraint: Thy love, O Christ, my Lord.
>
> My Confidence: Thou art able to keep that which I have committed unto thee.
>
> My Joy: To do Thy will, O God.
>
> My Discipline: That which I would not choose, but which Thy love appoints.

My Prayer: Conform my will to Thine.

My Motto: Love to live—live to love.

My Portion: The Lord is the portion of mine inheritance.

With that kind of devotion and dedication, is it any wonder that Amy Carmichael was misunderstood by believers, persecuted by unbelievers, attacked by Satan, and blessed by the Lord?

Unpredictable? Yes—*but not unblessable!* We could use a few more like her in Christian service today.

9

Oswald Chambers
1874–1917

"I feel I shall be buried for a time, hidden away in obscurity; then suddenly I shall flame out, do my work, and be gone."

Those words were spoken by Oswald Chambers, author of *My Utmost for His Highest* and more than thirty other books that never seem to grow old. His statement was prophetic—except that the flame God lit is still burning brightly, thanks to the printed page.

When you review the life of Oswald Chambers, you can well understand why a friend once introduced him as "the apostle of the haphazard." Like the wind Jesus spoke of in John 3:8, Chambers came and went in a seemingly erratic fashion; yet there was a definite plan in his life, and he was greatly used of God. He is a good reminder to boxed-in Christians that God sometimes bypasses our date-books and management-by-objectives and does the surprising, even the unexpected, in our lives.

Oswald Chambers was born in Aberdeen, Scotland, on July 24, 1874. His parents had been baptized by Charles Spurgeon, who had also ordained Chambers's father into Baptist ministry. While the family was living in London, teenage Oswald gave his heart to Christ.

He and his father were walking home from a meeting conducted by Spurgeon, and Oswald admitted that he would have given himself to the Lord had the opportunity been given. "You can do it now, my boy!" said his father, and right there, the boy trusted Christ and was born again. He was baptized by Rev. J. T. Briscoe and became a member of the Rye Lane Baptist Church in London.

A gifted artist, Chambers entered art school in 1892 and three years later went to Edinburgh to continue his studies. In 1896, he felt a definite call to the ministry, and the following year he entered the Dunoon Training College in Scotland. Not only did he have an outstanding record as a student, but he remained after graduation to teach. He had a special interest in philosophy and psychology, and taught those courses.

But in November 1901, Chambers had a deep experience with the Lord that transformed his life. He called it a baptism of the Holy Spirit, a term I prefer to apply only to the believer's experience at conversion (see 1 Cor. 12:13). This special filling of the Spirit gave him new insights into both the Christian life and the courses he was then teaching. In his ministry of the Word, he reveals both the philosopher and the psychologist.

He left school in 1905 and began an itinerant ministry in Britain, the United States, and Japan. He taught at the Oriental Missionary Society Bible School in Tokyo, and then he became a "missioner" for the League of Prayer that had been founded by Reader Harris. He was married on May 25, 1910, to Gertrude Hobbs, a devoted woman who was also an expert stenographer, a fact that would mean much in the years to come.

Chambers felt there was a need for a Bible college in Britain that would emphasize personal Christian living and not just education and practical training. With the help of some friends, he founded the Bible Training College at Clapham. The school operated on faith and prayer. When a friend offered to endow the school, Chambers refused the offer saying, "No, if you do that it will probably go on longer than God means it to."

He felt led to offer himself as a military chaplain during World War I, and on October 9, 1915, he sailed with the troops for Zeitoun, Egypt, where he ministered until his untimely death on November 15, 1917. He had appendicitis and did not know it; peritonitis set in and his life could not be saved.

At this point his wife Gertrude (whom everybody called Biddy) and his daughter Kathleen enter the picture and become very important. Biddy remained at their home in Zeitoun and ministered for about a year. Then she and her daughter returned to England. Over the years, she had taken stenographic reports of her husband's messages and, at the request of many friends, began to edit and publish them.

Oswald Chambers never actually wrote any of his books, although his name is on them. He spoke every word, but it was his wife, and later his daughter, who prepared the manuscripts and mothered each book through the presses. How grateful we are to God that Chambers married an expert stenographer!

His most famous book is *My Utmost for His Highest*, a daily devotional book that not every Christian can immediately appreciate. I recall telling a mature Christian friend many years ago that I was getting nothing out of the book. "Set it aside for a time," she counseled. "It's something you have to grow into." She was right: the problem was not the complexity of the book but the spiritual immaturity of the reader. In later years, I have come to appreciate this classic devotional book, and I learn more from it as the years go by.

Too many devotional books are finished with one reading, because they do not get down to the fundamental truths that keep expanding into more truth. A good book is like a seed: it produces fruit that has in it seed for more fruit. It is not a picture on the wall; it is a window that invites us to wider horizons.

Each time I read a page from *My Utmost for His Highest,* I am reminded of a forgotten nugget, or I see something new that previously had eluded me. It is a book to grow with and, as such, it is unique.

All the writings of Oswald Chambers have their value. I must confess that I get a bit tired of his alliteration, some of which seems forced, but I have learned to look beyond it. I have especially appreciated his book on Abraham, *Not*

Knowing Whither. The Philosophy of Sin has some penetrating insights in it. Chambers was similar to F. B. Meyer in his ability to diagnose spiritual problems and give biblical solutions. *Biblical Psychology* reveals Chambers the amateur psychologist, but the emphasis is on the Bible and not the psychology. His studies in Job, *Baffled to Fight Better*, are brief but rich, and very rewarding.

The official biography, *Oswald Chambers: His Life and Work*, was compiled and edited by his wife. She quoted from his journals, added her own comments, and quoted from material given her by his many friends and associates in ministry. Like Chambers himself, this book is a bit haphazard, and the reader can easily lose the chronological trail. But the many quotations from Chambers, and the revelation of his personality, make its reading worthwhile. It was published in London in 1933 by Simpkin Marshall, Ltd.

What kind of a man was Oswald Chambers? For one thing, he was not a brittle and pious "saint" who lived aloof from the world and the people around him. He was very much alive, and he had a marvelous sense of humor. One man wrote to Mrs. Chambers that he had been "shocked at what I then considered his undue levity. He was the most irreverent Reverend I had ever met!"

But Chambers gave himself totally to the Lord, and this included his sense of humor. He once wrote in his journal, "Lord, keep me radiantly and joyously Thine." En route to Egypt, he conducted services on the ship and brought his humor into the messages.

"Ah, I see," said one of the men, "your jokes and lightheart-edness plough the land, then you put in the seed." You could not find a better philosophy of humor in the pulpit than that.

Chambers emphasized holy living, but he did not divorce it from the practical affairs of life. "I am realizing more and more the futility of separating a life into secular and sacred. It is all His." Those words summarize his position perfectly. He wrote to a friend, "You can be much more for Him than ever you know by just being yourself and relying on Him. . . . Keep praying and playing and being yourself." He felt that his own greatest ministry was that of intercessory prayer.

A gifted teacher, he was careful that the truths he taught were meaningful in his own life. "Views from propagandist teaching are borrowed plumes," he said. "Teaching is meant to stir up thinking, not to store with goods from the out-side." That is good counsel in this age when many teachers and preachers manufacture their lessons and sermons out of borrowed nuggets instead of mining their own gold and refining it in experience.

Chambers sought to present truth in ways that would ex-cite new interest in his listeners. One listener said, "I won-dered, as I drank in his message, whether I had the same Bible as he had. The written Word became a Living Word, and as I obeyed it my whole life was altered."

He would have agreed with A. W. Tozer that the only *real* world is the world of truth found in the Bible. He wrote: "The Actual world of things and the Real world of Truth have to be made into one in personal experience." Too many Christians try to avoid this creative tension by going either to extreme isolation from the world or to extreme preoccupation with the world.

Oswald Chambers loved books and read widely. The biography contains references to many authors of different theological positions, from Alexander Maclaren and John Henry Jowett to Emmanuel Swedenborg and Ralph Waldo Emerson. "My books!" he wrote to a friend. "I cannot tell you what they are to me—silent, wealthy, loyal lovers. . . . I do thank God for my books with every fiber of my being. Friends that are ever true and ever your own." He always integrated his wide reading with the Word of God, which he considered the only test for spiritual truth.

In many respects, Chambers was not in tune with the general spirit of evangelical Christianity in his day. On his way to Egypt, he wrote in his journal: "How unproselytizing God is! I feel the 'soul winning campaign' is often at heart the apotheosis [glorification] of commercialism, the desire to see so much result from so much expenditure. The ordinary evangelical spirit is less and less congenial to my own soul." His writings are a good antidote to the success philosophy that has invaded the church in our own day. He said that "the 'soul saving passion' as an aim must cease and merge into the passion for Christ, revealing itself in holiness in all human relationships." In other words, soul-winning is not something we *do*, it is something we *are*, twenty-four hours a day, and we live for souls because we love Christ. No counting trophies in his ministry.

He was not afraid to accept truth no matter what channel God might use to give it to him. He told students to "*soak,*

soak, soak in philosophy and psychology. . . . It is ignorance of the subjects on the part of ministers and workers that has brought our evangelical theology to such a sorry plight."[1] Both in the pulpit and classroom, and as a personal counselor, Chambers revealed his keen understanding of the Bible, the human heart and mind, and the world of thought. He was able to blend these disciplines into a total ministry that God greatly used.

Let me share a few quotations from Oswald Chambers that, I trust, will whet your appetite for more.

> You can never give another person that which you have found, but you can make him homesick for what you have.

> If we are saved and sanctified, God guides us by our ordinary choices, and if we are going to choose what He does not want, He will check, and we must heed.

> Every doctrine that is not imbedded in the Cross of Jesus will lead astray.

> Stop having a measuring rod for other people. There is always one fact more in every man's case about which we know nothing.

> It takes a long time to realize the danger of being an amateur providence, that is, interfering with God's order for others.

> Our Lord's first obedience was to the will of His Father, not to the needs of men; the saving of men was the natural outcome of His obedience to the Father.[2]

One of his sayings that is underlined in my copy of *My Utmost for His Highest* has been especially meaningful to me.

> The snare in Christian work is to rejoice in successful service, to rejoice in the fact that God has used you. . . . If you make usefulness the test, then Jesus Christ was the greatest failure that ever lived. The lodestar of the saint is God Himself, not estimated usefulness. It is the work that God does through us that counts, not what we do for Him.[3]

Mrs. Chambers died in 1966, just after she had begun to prepare the thirty-second volume for the publishers, and her daughter completed the book. How grateful to God we should be for Biddy and Kathleen's unselfish labor of love over the years, in sharing the ministry of Oswald Chambers with us. His body is buried in the cemetery in Old Cairo, his spirit is rejoicing in the presence of God, and his ministry goes on triumphantly.

Perhaps one final quotation will sum up his philosophy of the Christian life. "Never make a principle out of your own experience; let God be as original with other people as He is with you."

He may have been the apostle of the haphazard, but Oswald Chambers can assist any sincere Christian in ordering his life according to the will of God.

10

A. W. Tozer
1897–1963

From 1928 to 1959, A. W. Tozer pastored Southside Alliance Church in Chicago and functioned as the conscience of evangelicalism at large. I heard him preach many times—always with profit—and waited for his books to be published as impatiently as a detective-story addict waits for the next installment of the current serial. I still reread his books regularly, and always find in them something new to think about. This does not mean I always agreed with Tozer. There were times when I felt he was leading a parade of one down a dead-end street, such as when he vigorously opposed Christian movies. His sometimes acid criticisms of new Bible translations and of churches that "majored in counting noses" were but small defects in an otherwise straight and sturdy wall. There was an intensity about his preaching, as there is about his writing. Tozer walked with God and knew him intimately.

To listen to Tozer preach was as safe as opening the door of a blast furnace!

To prevent a generation arising that knows not Tozer, I want to devote the first half of this chapter to the man and his books, then I want to consider some other Christian mystics.

The official biography of Tozer is written by David J. Fant Jr. and is entitled *A. W. Tozer: A Twentieth-Century Prophet*. Unfortunately, the book does not tell too much about the man, and what it does tell might have been written for a press release or for page one of an appreciation booklet. The first chapter takes us from his birth (April 21, 1897) to his death (May 12, 1963), and the remaining eleven chapters concentrate on Tozer's writing, summarizing what he believed and why he believed it. If I understand Tozer's philosophy of books and writing, he would disagree with Fant's approach. "Read the man himself!" he would say. "Don't read *about* the man, or what some writer says about the man. Read the man himself!" While I appreciate the excellent quotations Fant selected and agree with his analysis of Tozer's thinking, I still feel that getting acquainted with this vibrant writer via a biographer is like going to a flower show over the telephone. I suggest you read Tozer's books first, then read Fant's biography.

Begin with *The Pursuit of God*, one of the best devotional books ever written by an American pastor. As your grandmother used to say about her home medicines, "It's good for what ails you!" *The Pursuit of God* polishes the lenses of my soul and helps me see better. It cures the fever that often makes a man mistake activity for ministry. It rebukes my lack of worship. For these reasons (and many more), I try to read the book at least once a year. Follow with *The Divine Conquest*, then with *The Knowledge of the Holy*, a book that, to me, is the finest modern devotional treatment of the attributes of God. Once you have read these three volumes, you will have a grasp of the essentials of Tozer's thinking about God, Christ, the Holy Spirit, the church, the Bible, and the responsibility of the believer in today's world. You are then prepared to launch into his books of spiritual essays, such as *The Root of the Righteous, Born After Midnight, Of God and Men, That Incredible Christian, Man: The Dwelling Place of God*, and (if you enjoy poetry and hymnody) *The Christian Book of Mystical Verse*. All of his books are published by Christian Publications, with the exception of *The Knowledge of the Holy*, which is published by Harper. Nearly all of these essays originally appeared as editorials in *The Alliance Witness*, which Tozer edited for many years and which was perhaps the only evangelical publication people read primarily for the editorials!

Let me suggest that you *not* read these books the way you read other books—attempting to finish them quickly, perhaps in one sitting (a phrase Tozer despised). Read Tozer leisurely, meditatively, almost as a worship experience. Read each essay slowly, as though the writer were chatting with you personally, in front of the friendly fireplace in his living room. Read with your heart; keep your ear tuned to that "other voice" that will surely speak to you and remind you of the truths of God's Word. My experience has been that, when reading a book by Tozer, some passage will cause me to put down the book, pick up my Bible, and then start thinking about some truth on my own. And this is exactly what Tozer would want! "The best book is not one that informs merely," he wrote, "but one that stirs the reader up to inform himself."[1] I try to keep a notebook at hand when I read any book, but especially when I read Tozer.

After becoming acquainted with his devotional essays, read the two biographies he wrote: *Wingspread*, the life of A. B. Simpson, founder of the Christian and Missionary Alliance, and *Let My People Go!* the life of missionary Robert A. Jaffray. Then investigate the volumes of sermons that have recently appeared, edited by Gerald B. Smith. Frankly, this series does not excite me. I can hear Tozer *in* these messages, but I believe he would have edited this material differently. I fear this may be prejudice on my part, but I prefer the incisiveness of the essays to the expansiveness of the sermons. But, since they are "genuine Tozer," I have them on my shelf and I read them.

Aiden Wilson Tozer (he preferred his initials, and who can blame him) considered himself an "evangelical mystic." Unfortunately the word *mystic* has never been a popular word in the evangelical vocabulary, especially in this day of activism and statistics. To most evangelicals, a mystic is an odd person who sees visions and hears voices and is about as useful to the church as a spare tire on a bobsled. If that were what mysticism is, I would want no part of it. But that is *not* mysticism; it is only a caricature of it. A mystic is simply a person who: (1) sees a real spiritual world beyond the world of sense, (2) seeks to please God rather than the crowd, (3) cultivates a close fellowship with God, sensing his presence everywhere, and (4) relates his experience to the practical things of life.

In his preface to *The Christian Book of Mystical Verse*, Tozer put it this way:

> I refer to the evangelical mystic who has been brought by the gospel into intimate fellowship with the Godhead. His theology is no less and no more than is taught in the Christian Scriptures. . . . He differs from the ordinary orthodox Christian only because he experiences his faith down in the depths of his sentient being while the other does not. He exists in a world of spiritual reality. He is quietly, deeply and sometimes almost ecstatically aware of the presence of God in his own nature and in the world around him. His religious experience is something elemental, as old as time and the creation. It is immediate acquaintance with God by union with the eternal son.[2]

Tozer's essay "Bible Taught or Spirit Taught?" is a good summary of his views on practical mysticism: "It is altogether possible to be instructed in the rudiments of the faith and still have no real understanding of the whole thing," he wrote. "And it is possible to go on to become expert in Bible doctrine and not have spiritual illumination, with the result that a veil remains over the mind, preventing it from apprehending the truth in its spiritual essence."[3] Tozer's sermons often confront us with these questions: Is God *real* to you? Is your Christian experience a set of definitions, a list of orthodox doctrines, or a living relationship with God? Do you have a firsthand experience with him, or a secondhand experience through others? Is your heart hungering and thirsting after personal holiness? These questions are applicable today, perhaps more than we dare to admit.

Fant, at the end of his biography, listed the books and authors that most influenced Tozer, and this list is something of a basic bibliography on the mystics. I am sure that many evangelical pastors today have either never been exposed to this wealth of devotional writing or have purposely avoided it, so I recommend the list to you. However, before you spend your book budget in securing these volumes, I suggest that you sample them in a manner that is quite easy and (best of all) inexpensive. *The Upper Room* (Nashville, Tennessee) publishes a series of attractive, pocket-size booklets called "The Great Devotional Classics." I believe there are thirty titles in the series, ranging from William Law (who strongly influenced the Wesleys) to William Temple (archbishop of Canterbury until his death in 1944). I suggest you carry one of these booklets with you to read in spare minutes. Each booklet contains from thirty to forty pages; there is a biographical introduction and a brief discussion of the influence of the writer (or the book) in church history. The thirty or more writers (or titles, where the writers are anonymous) cover a wide spectrum of theological and ecclesiastical groups.

You will find John Knox, prophet of the Reformation in Scotland; François Fenelon, close friend to Madame Guyon; George Fox, founder of the Quakers; John Wesley and Francis Asbury, the great Methodist leaders; Henry Scougal, whose *Life of God in the Soul of Man* is easily the greatest devotional work to come out of Scotland; Søren Kierkegaard, the melancholy Danish philosopher; Dietrich Bonhoeffer, the German theologian; and even Thomas Kelly, the young Quaker writer whose untimely death halted an exciting career. There are selections from anonymous works: *Theologia Germanica*, which Luther put alongside the Bible and Augustine's writings, and *Cloud of Unknowing*, which Tozer loved to quote.

If you profit from this excursion into the land of Christian mysticism, then search for another volume that must be on your devotional shelf. Unfortunately, like many fine books, it is out of print. Abingdon Press ought to reissue this book and make it available to this generation of preachers. I refer to *The Fellowship of the Saints*, an anthology of devotional writings edited by Thomas S. Kepler, for many years professor at Oberlin College. Kepler was an ardent student of the mystics, and in this large (800-page) volume he gives the best of their writings in a chronological sequence that enables the reader to trace the influence of one writer on the next. He starts with Clement of Rome and ends with selections from twentieth-century writers. To be sure, there is some chaff here; but there is so much fine wheat that the chaff does not upset me. Look for a copy in used-book stores; I hope you find one!

Kepler compiled another anthology that you may want to secure: *The Evelyn Underhill Reader*. Evelyn Underhill was a well-known British mystic who died in 1941. Her books, *Mysticism, Practical Mysticism,* and *Worship* are almost standard texts on these subjects. Unfortunately she was never quite sure of her theology, and it is here she parts company with

Tozer. She confessed to being "a modernist on many points." But some of her personal insights are helpful, and therefore she should be read. Like poison, these matters should be "handled" but not permitted into one's system!

Harper and Row has published two basic books that should be in your library: *Christian Perfection*, written by François Fenelon and published in 1947, and *Treatises and Sermons of Meister Eckhart*, published in 1958. Fenelon's book is priceless for devotional reading—a chapter a day. Here is a man who conducted "spiritual conferences" in the court of Louis XIV! Chapter 1 is "On the Use of Time" and is one of the finest treatments of this elusive subject, from a spiritual point of view, that you will find anywhere. Chapter 2 deals with "Recreation." Chapter 8 considers "Fidelity in Little Things." Every pastor will want to read chapter 14, "Dryness and Distraction." These chapters are not long, but they are deep and profoundly practical. I cannot recommend this book too highly. Eckhart was a German mystic (1260–1327) whose purity of life gave great power to his preaching. Selections from his many writings are available in different editions, the most popular of which is probably *After Supper in the Refectory: A Series of Instructions*, published in 1917. Tozer recommended this book. The volume referred to above contains selections from *Talks of Instruction* as well as material from other writings.

If you wish to purchase a copy of *Cloud of Unknowing*, the edition edited by Evelyn Underhill is perhaps the best. The introduction by the editor and the glossary of terms are both very helpful to those not conversant with mystical writings.

However, I must confess that, so far, this book has failed to reach me, although here and there some statements have struck fire. The repeated phrase "O Ghostly friend in God" still makes me chuckle. Out of respect for the anonymous author, I try to chuckle in a mystical way, but I fear I do not always succeed. As I grow spiritually, I am sure I will better appreciate this book.

The mystics wrote to cultivate the inner man, and certainly this is a neglected activity in our churches today. We have more Marthas than Marys! But, in the long run, the ideal Christian will not be one or the other: he will be a balance of both. Worship and work will not compete; they will cooperate. This is the contribution the evangelical mystics can make to our lives, and I trust you will sincerely give them the opportunity to do so.

Martyn Lloyd-Jones and I were discussing the mystics over dinner one evening, and he related an interesting experience. With his permission I repeat it here.

"Dr. Tozer and I shared a conference years ago," he said, "and I appreciated his ministry and his fellowship very much. One day he said to me, 'Lloyd-Jones, you and I hold just about the same position on spiritual matters, but we have come to this position by different routes.'

"'How do you mean?' I asked.

"'Well,' Tozer replied, 'you came by way of the Puritans and I came by way of the mystics.' And, you know, he was right!"

Which perhaps goes to prove that doctrine and devotion have been joined together by God and that no man dare put them asunder. Our understanding of doctrine ought to lead us into greater devotion to Christ, and our deeper devotion ought to make us better servants and soul-winners. Jesus beautifully joined both together when he said: "Abide in me and I in you . . . for without me, ye can do nothing." This is the message of the evangelical mystics, a message we desperately need to hear today.

Further Reading

Matthew Henry

Henry, Matthew. *Matthew Henry's Commentary on the Whole Bible: Complete and Unabridged*. Peabody, MS: Hendrickson Publishers, 2005.

Williams, J. B. *The Life of Matthew Henry and the Concise Commentary on the Gospels*. Alachua, FL: Bridge-Logos Publishers, 2004.

———. *The Lives of Philip and Matthew Henry*. London: Banner of Truth Trust, 1974.

Jonathan Edwards

Dwight, Sereno E. "Memoirs of Jonathan Edwards" in *The Works of Jonathan Edwards*, vol. 1. Edinburgh: Banner of Truth Trust, 1974.

Marsden, George M. *Jonathan Edwards: A Life*. New Haven: Yale University Press, 2004.

Murray, Iain. *Jonathan Edwards: A New Biography*. Edinburgh: Banner of Truth Trust, 1987.

Nichols, Stephen J. *Jonathan Edwards: A Guided Tour of His Life and Thought*. Phillipsburg, NJ: P & R Press, 2001.

Stein, Stephen J. *The Cambridge Companion to Jonathan Edwards*. Cambridge: Cambridge University Press, 2006.

John Henry Newman

Church, R. W. *The Oxford Movement, Twelve Years, 1833–1845.* London: Macmillan, 1891. Reprint, New York: Archon, 1966.

Newman, John Henry. *Apologia pro vita sua.* London: Longmans, 1864. Reprint edited by David J. DeLaura. New York: Norton, 1968.

———. *Discourses Addressed to Mixed Congregations.* London: Longmans, 1849. Reprint, Westminster, MD: Christian Classics, 1966.

———. *Lectures and Essays on University Subjects.* London: Longman, Brown, Green, Longmans, and Roberts, 1859.

———. *A Newman Reader: An Anthology of the Writings of John Henry Cardinal Newman.* Edited by Francis X. Connolly. Garden City, NY: Doubleday, 1964.

———. *Parochial and Plain Sermons.* Edited by W. J. Copeland. 8 vols. London: Rivingtons, 1868. Reprint, Westminster, MD: Christian Classics, 1968.

———. *The Preaching of John Henry Newman.* Edited by W. D. White. Philadelphia: Fortress, 1969.

———. *Sermons Bearing on Subjects of the Day.* London: Rivingtons, 1843. Reprint, Westminster, MD: Christian Classics, 1968.

———. *Sermons, Chiefly on the Theory of Religious Belief, Preached Before the University of Oxford.* London: Rivingtons, 1843. Reprinted as *Fifteen Sermons Preached Before the University of Oxford, Between AD 1826 and 1843.* Westminster, MD: Christian Classics, 1970.

———. *Sermons Preached on Various Occasions.* London: Burns and Lambert, 1857. Reprint, Westminster, MD: Christian Classics, 1968.

———. *Tract Ninety; or, Remarks on Certain Passages in the Thirty-Nine Articles.* Edited by A. W. Evans. London: Constable, 1933.

Nicoll, W. Robertson. *Princes of the Church.* London: Hodder and Stoughton, 1921.

O'Connell, Marvin R. *The Oxford Conspirators: A History of the Oxford Movement, 1833–45.* New York: Macmillan, 1969.

Trevor, Meriol. *Newman.* 2 vols.: *The Pillar of the Cloud and Light in Winter.* New York: Macmillan, 1962–63.

————. *Newman's Journey*. Cleveland: Collins and World, 1977.

Turner, Frank M., and Frank Turner. *John Henry Newman: The Challenge to Evangelical Religion*. New Haven: Yale University Press, 2002.

Whyte, Alexander. *Newman: An Appreciation in Two Lectures, with the Choicest Passages of His Writings*. Edinburgh: Oliphant, 1901.

J. B. Lightfoot

Bishop Lightfoot. London: Macmillan, 1894.

Eden, George R., and F. C. Macdonald, eds. *Lightfoot of Durham: Memories and Appreciations*. Cambridge: Cambridge University, 1932.

Lightfoot, J. B. *The Apostolic Fathers*. Edited by J. R. Harmer. London: Macmillan, 1891. Reprint, Grand Rapids: Baker, 1956.

————. *Cambridge Sermons*. London: Macmillan, 1890.

————. *Commentary on the Epistles of St. Paul*. 43 vols. London: Macmillan, 1865–75. Reprint, Peabody, MA: Hendrickson Publishers, 1993.

————. *Historical Essays*. London: Macmillan, 1895.

————. *Leaders in the Northern Church*. Edited by J. R. Harmer. London: Macmillan, 1890.

————. *On a Fresh Revision of the English New Testament*. London: Cambridge, 1871.

————. *Ordination Addresses and Counsels to Clergy*. London: Macmillan, 1890.

————. *Sermons Preached in St. Paul's Cathedral*. London: Macmillan, 1891.

————. *Sermons Preached on Special Occasions*. London: Macmillan, 1891.

Nicoll, W. Robertson. *Princes of the Church*. London: Hodder and Stoughton, 1921.

J. Hudson Taylor

Cromarty, Jim. *The Pigtail and Chopsticks Man: The Story of J. Hudson Taylor and the China Inland Mission*. Darlington, UK: Evangelical Press, 2002.

Pollock, John Charles. *Hudson Taylor and Maria*. New York: McGraw-Hill, 1962.

Steer, Roger. *J. Hudson Taylor: A Man in Christ*. Carlisle, UK: Authentic, 1969.

————. *Hudson Taylor*. Bloomington: Bethany House Publishers, 1987.

Taylor, Howard, and Mary Taylor. *Biography of James Hudson Taylor*. London: China Inland Mission, 1965. Reprinted as *J. Hudson Taylor: God's Man in China*. Chicago: Moody, 1971.

————. *Hudson Taylor and the China Inland Mission: The Growth of a Work of God*. London: Morgan and Scott, 1918.

————. *Hudson Taylor in Early Years: The Growth of a Soul*. London: Morgan and Scott, 1911.

Taylor, J. Hudson. *Hudson Taylor's Legacy*. Edited by Marshall Broomhall. London: China Inland Mission, 1931.

————. *A Retrospect*. London: Morgan, 1894.

————. *Union and Communion*. London: Morgan and Scott, 1894. Reprint, Minneapolis: Bethany Fellowship, 1971.

Charles H. Spurgeon

Bacon, Ernest W. *Spurgeon: Heir of the Puritans*. Grand Rapids: Eerdmans, 1968.

Booth, Bramwell. *Echoes and Memories*. New York: Doran, 1925.

Fullerton, W. Y. *C. H. Spurgeon*. London: Williams and Norgate, 1920. Reprint, Chicago: Moody, 1966.

Hayden, Eric W. *A History of Spurgeon's Tabernacle*. 2nd ed. Pasadena, TX: Pilgrim, 1971.

Murray, Iain. *The Forgotten Spurgeon*. 2nd ed. London: Banner of Truth Trust, 1973.

Spurgeon, Charles H. *All of Grace*. Christian Heritage, 2008.

————. *An All-Round Ministry*. London: Passmore and Alabaster, 1900. Reprint, Pasadena, TX: Pilgrim Ministry.

————. *Autobiography*. Edited by Susannah Spurgeon and Joseph Harrald. 4 vols. London: Passmore and Alabaster, 1897–1900. Reprinted as *Spurgeon*. 2 vols. Edinburgh: Banner of Truth Trust, 1962–73.

————. *Commenting and Commentaries*. London: Passmore and Alabaster, 1876. Reprint, London: Banner of Truth Trust, 1969.

————. *Lectures to My Students*. 3 vols. London: Passmore and Alabaster, 1875–94. Reprint, 1 vol. London: Marshall, Morgan, and Scott, 1954.

————. *The Metropolitan Tabernacle Pulpit*. 56 vols. London: Passmore and Alabaster, 1863ff. Reprint, Pasadena, TX: Pilgrim Ministry.

————. *Morning and Evening: A New Edition of the Classic Devotional*. Revised and updated edition. Wheaton: Crossway Books, 2003.

Thielicke, Helmut. *Encounter with Spurgeon*. Philadelphia: Fortress, 1963. Reprint, Grand Rapids: Baker, 1975.

Dwight L. Moody

Curtis, Richard K. *They Called Him Mr. Moody*. Grand Rapids: Eerdmans, 1962.

Day, Richard Ellsworth. *Bush Aglow*. Philadelphia: The Judson Press, 1936.

Findlay, James F., Jr. *Dwight L. Moody; American Evangelist*. Reprint, Grand Rapids: Baker, 1973.

Fitt, Arthur Percy. *Moody Still Lives*. New York: Revell, 1936.

Gundry, Stanley N. *Love Them In: The Proclamation Theology of D. L. Moody*. Chicago: Moody, 1976.

Moody, William R. *The Life of Dwight L. Moody*. New York: Revell, 1900.

Pollock, J. C. *Moody without Sankey*. London: Hodder and Stoughton, 1963.

Smith, Wilbur M. *An Annotated Bibliography of D. L. Moody*. Chicago: Moody, 1948.

Williams, A. W. *Life and Work of Dwight L. Moody*. New York: Cosimo Classics, 2006.

Amy Carmichael

Benge, Janet and Geoff Benge. *Amy Carmichael: Rescuer of Precious Gems.* Seattle: YWAM, 1998.

Carmichael, Amy. *I Come Quietly to Meet You: An Intimate Journey in God's Presence.* Bloomington, MN: Bethany House Publishers, 2005.

Eliot, Elisabeth. *A Chance To Die: The Life and Legacy of Amy Carmichael.* Old Tappan, NJ: Revell, 1987. Reprint, Grand Rapids: Revell, 2005.

Houghton, Frank. *Amy Carmichael of Dohnavur.* London: SPCK, 1953. Reprint, Fort Washington, PA: Christian Literature Crusade, 1988.

Oswald Chambers

Chambers, Gertrude H. *Oswald Chambers: His Life and Work.* London: Simpkin Marshall, Ltd., 1933.

Chambers, Oswald. *The Complete Works of Oswald Chambers.* Compiled by Biddy Chambers. Grand Rapids: Discovery House, 2000.

———. *If You Will Ask.* Grand Rapids: Discovery House, 1994.

———. *Love: A Holy Command.* Grand Rapids: Discovery House, 2008.

McCasland, David. *Oswald Chambers: Abandoned to God.* Grand Rapids: Discovery House, 1993.

Verploegh, Harry, ed. *Oswald Chambers: The Best from All the Books.* 2 vols. Nashville: Thomas Nelson, 1987, 1989.

A. W. Tozer

Anonymous. *Cloud of Unknowing: A Book of Contemplation.* Edited by Evelyn Underhill. London: Watkins, 1970.

Dorsett, Lyle. *A Passion for God: The Spiritual Journey of A.W. Tozer.* Chicago: Moody, 2008.

Eckhart, Meister. *After Supper in the Refectory: A Series of Instructions.* Translated by N. Leeson. London: Mowbray, 1917.

———. *Treatises and Sermons.* Edited and translated by James M. Clark and John V. Skinner. New York: Harper, 1958.

Fant, David J., Jr. *A. W. Tozer: A Twentieth-Century Prophet.* Harrisburg, PA: Christian Publications, 1964.

Fenelon, François. *Christian Perfection.* Edited by Charles F. Whiston. Translated by Mildred Whitney Stillman. New York: Harper, 1947.

Kepler, Thomas S., ed. *The Fellowship of the Saints.* New York: Abingdon, 1948.

Snyder, James L. *The Life of A.W. Tozer: In Pursuit of God.* Ventura, CA: Regal Books, 2009.

Tozer, A. W. *Born After Midnight.* Harrisburg, PA: Christian Publications, 1964.

———, ed. *The Christian Book of Mystical Verse.* Harrisburg, PA: Christian Publications, 1963.

———. *The Divine Conquest.* Harrisburg, PA: Christian Publications, 1950.

———. *The Root of the Righteous.* Harrisburg, PA: Christian Publications, 1955.

———. *The Knowledge of the Holy: The Attributes of God.* New York: Harper, 1961.

———. *Let My People Go! The Life of Robert A. Jaffray.* Harrisburg, PA: Christian Publications, 1947.

———. *Man: The Dwelling Place of God.* Harrisburg, PA: Christian Publications, 1966.

———. *Of God and Men.* Harrisburg, PA: Christian Publications, 1960.

———. *The Pursuit of God.* Harrisburg, PA: Christian Publications, 1948.

———. *That Incredible Christian.* Harrisburg, PA: Christian Publications, 1964.

———. *Tozer on Worship and Entertainment.* Camp Hill, PA: WingSpread Publishers, 2006.

———. *The Tozer Pulpit.* Edited by Gerald B. Smith. Harrisburg, PA: Christian Publications, 1967.

———. *Wingspread: Albert B. Simpson.* Harrisburg, PA: Christian Publications, 1943.

Underhill, Evelyn. *The Evelyn Underhill Reader.* Edited by Thomas S. Kepler. New York: Abingdon, 1962.

Notes

Chapter 1 Matthew Henry

1. C. H. Spurgeon, *Commenting and Commentaries* (London: Banner of Truth Trust, 1969), 3.

Chapter 2 Jonathan Edwards

1. Jonathan Edwards, *Works of Jonathan Edwards*, vol. 1 (London: Banner of Truth Trust, 1976), 237.

Chapter 3 John Henry Newman

1. W. Robertson Nicoll, *Princes of the Church* (London: Hodder and Stoughton, 1921), 29.

2. Alexander Whyte, *Newman: An Appreciation in Two Lectures, with the Choicest Passages of His Writings* (Edinburgh: Oliphant, 1901), 122.

3. Ibid., 90–92, 97.

4. R. W. Church, *The Oxford Movement, Twelve Years, 1833–1845* (London: Macmillan, 1891; repr., New York: Archon, 1966), 15.

5. John Henry Newman, *Lectures and Essays on University Subjects* (London: Longman, Brown, Green, Longmans, and Roberts, 1859), 218.

Chapter 4 J. B. Lightfoot

1. W. Robertson Nicoll, *The Victorian Church*, 2 vols. (London: Black, 1966), 2:49.

2. Nicoll, *Princes of the Church*, 22.

3. Ibid., 23.

Chapter 5 J. Hudson Taylor

1. Howard Taylor and Mary Taylor, *Hudson Taylor in Early Years: The Growth of a Soul* (London: Morgan and Scott, 1911), xvii.

2. John Charles Pollock, *Hudson Taylor and Maria* (New York: McGraw-Hill, 1962), 101.

3. Ibid., 202–3.

4. Howard Taylor and Mary Taylor, *Hudson Taylor and the China Inland Mission* (London: Morgan and Scott, 1918), 42.

5. Ibid., 54–55.

6. Ibid., 53.

7. Ibid., 461.

Chapter 6 Charles H. Spurgeon

1. Charles H. Spurgeon, *The Metropolitan Tabernacle Pulpit*, 56 vols. (London: Passmore and Alabaster, 1863ff), 10:573ff.

2. W. Y. Fullerton, *C. H. Spurgeon* (London: Williams and Norgate, 1920; repr., Chicago: Moody, 1966), 255.

3. Bramwell Booth, *Echoes and Memories* (New York: Doran, 1925), 34.

4. Lewis A. Drummond, *Spurgeon: Prince of Preachers* (Grand Rapids: Kregel, 1992), 675, 733–37. *See also* Fullerton, *C. H. Spurgeon*, 243–47.

Chapter 7 Dwight L. Moody

1. L. T. Remlap, ed., *The Gospel Awakening* (Chicago: J. Fairbanks and Co., n.d.), 90–91.

2. Sarah A. Cooke, *Wayside Sketches* (Grand Rapids: Shaw Publishing Co., n.d.), 50.

3. Stanley N. Gundry, *Love Them In* (Chicago: Moody, 1976), 153–54.

Chapter 9 Oswald Chambers

1. Gertrude Chambers, *Oswald Chambers: His Life and Work* (London: Simpkin Marshall, Ltd., 1933), 132.

2. Harry Verploegh, ed., *The Oswald Chambers Devotional Reader* (Nashville: Thomas Nelson, 1990). *See also Faith, A Holy Walk* compiled by Julie Ackerman Link (Grand Rapids: Discovery House, 1999).

3. David McCasland, ed., *The Quotable Oswald Chambers* (Grand Rapids: Discovery House, 2008).

Chapter 10 A. W. Tozer

1. A. W. Tozer, "Some Thoughts on Books and Reading," in *Man: The Dwelling Place of God* (Harrisburg, PA: Christian Publications, 1966), 149.

2. A. W. Tozer, ed. *The Christian Book of Mystical Verse* (Harrisburg, PA: Christian Publications, 1963), vi.

3. A. W. Tozer, *In The Root of the Righteous* (Harrisburg, PA: Christian Publications, 1955), 34–37.

Warren W. Wiersbe is a pastor and author or compiler of more than 150 books, including *50 People Every Christian Should Know*, *On Earth as It Is in Heaven*, and *Through the Year with Warren W. Wiersbe*. Today his primary ministry is serving others through writing. He lives in Nebraska.

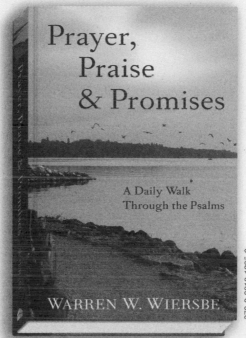

Find STRENGTH in their STORIES.

978-0-8010-7194-2

We all need inspiration to lead lives that honor God. When our faith is weak or the pressures of the world seem overwhelming, remembering the great men and women of the past can inspire us to renewed strength and purpose. Our spiritual struggles are not new, and the stories of those who have gone before can help lead the way to our own victories.

50 People Every Christian Should Know gives a glimpse into the lives of people such as:

- Charles H.
  Spurgeon
- A. W. Tozer
- Jonathan Edwards
- G. Campbell
  Morgan
- Amy Carmichael
- Fanny Crosby
- James Hudson
  Taylor

BakerBooks

Relevant. Intelligent. Engaging.

Available at bookstores, online at www.bakerbooks.com, or by calling (800) 877-2665.

Like us on ▪ Follow us on ▪ ReadBakerBooks Baker Books Blog: relligent.wordpress.com